HANDSOME
HEROINES

3—

Shahrukh Husain

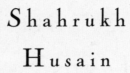

ANCHOR BOOKS

Doubleday

New York   London
Toronto   Sydney
Auckland

HANDSOME HEROINES

*Women
as Men
in Folklore*

AN ANCHOR BOOK
PUBLISHED BY DOUBLEDAY
a division of Bantam Doubleday Dell Publishing Group, Inc.
1540 Broadway, New York, New York 10036

ANCHOR BOOKS, DOUBLEDAY, and the portrayal of an anchor
are trademarks of Doubleday, a division of
Bantam Doubleday Dell Publishing Group, Inc.

Handsome Heroines was originally published in hardcover as *Women Who Wear the
Breeches* by Virago Press Limited in 1995. The Anchor Books edition is published by
arrangement with Virago Press Limited.

Book design by Maria Carella

Library of Congress Cataloging-in-Publication Data
Shahrukh Husain.
[Women who wear the breeches]
Handsome heroines : women as men in folklore / Shahrukh Husain.
p.   cm.
Originally published: Women who wear the breeches :
United Kingdom : Virago, 1995.
Includes bibliographical references.
1. Fairy tales—Adaptations.   2. Transvestites—Fiction.
3. Women—Fiction.   I. Title.
PR6069.H283W66   1996
823'.914—dc20   96-12169
CIP

ISBN 0-385-48405-4

October 1996

1   3   5   7   9   10   8   6   4   2

First U.S. Edition

For
Ruth Petrie

ACKNOWLEDGMENTS

To Lennie Goodings, my editor, for her patience and for her insightful comments and advice, particularly on the introduction. To Christopher Shackle, my husband, for his tireless detective work in following up leads for my stories in libraries, bookstores, and flea markets, and to Mary Ann Hushlak for her encouragement throughout. Most of all to my daughter, Samira, who read all the stories and suggested some of the titles. Also to the library staff at the Folklore Society Library, who went out of their way to help me locate material.

CONTENTS

INTRODUCTION

I was ten when I heard my first tale of a woman dressed as a man. It told of a blacksmith's daughter who married a reckless young king, then dressed herself as a man to rescue him from a wicked princess.

I found the feisty blacksmith's daughter compelling with her irrepressible zest for life. She was determined to command her husband's respect. She was willing to play life at its own game. There was a deliciously "do-what-thou-wilt" quality about her. She pushed risk to its limits. She was an opportunist who used every advantage within her grasp, laughing her way to success. She triumphed and I was hooked.

The blacksmith's daughter did the things that I as a child had already been told were wrong but that continued to tantalize my child's heart. She answered back, she was willful and disobedient, she lied and cheated. She was the bad girl incarnate, the type grown-ups would have told me not to mix with. And what fun she had living dangerously!

The story came from a fierce-looking frontiersman who was temporarily replacing the night watchman in our family home in Karachi, and he was unreservedly delighted by the heroine's romps—the taunting, the cheating, and the ultimate defeat of her husband. Admittedly, his version did not stress the fact that when the blacksmith's daughter returned to the king, it was on different terms. He ended with the king's apology, but his tone and his demeanor showed that he was thrilled by her victory.

In retrospect, I realize that the frontiersman told the story with such gusto and vibrancy because he identified with the heroine. He and she became interchangeable as he referred to her now in the masculine, now in the feminine, simultaneously sustaining both female and male personae. She was the perfect androgyne, representing the protective and the assertive in male and female. And the question of what became of the princess, or why her husband had failed to recognize her in spite of being her groom, was a peripheral issue—listener and teller were focused entirely on the heroine's need, cheering her on in her determination to fulfill it.

I mined the library shelves for others like her and found cross-dressers in many places from Enid Blyton to Shakespeare, in China, Africa, Europe, and the Middle East, in literature, modern fiction, and in history. But none was remotely as exciting and daring as the irresistible, anarchic cross-dresser of fairy tales. It made my search more thrilling over the years as I plucked the stories one by one from the memories of storytellers and from various anthologies until I had gathered a substantial collection of this strand of the fairy tale that celebrates the many inclinations of woman—from duty to betrayal, from honesty to fraudulence, from devotion to irreverence.

Around the world, tales of cross-dressers are rich and diverse, but in time I came to see some story clusters: stories from the East, for example, tend to feature aristocratic heroines who embark on the traditional fairy-tale quest, battling with monsters and demons, while in northern Europe women favor dressing in uniform, fighting wars, and sailing the seas. Some women risk their lives by choosing the ascetic's path, others, particularly in the Italian novellas, are forced into monk's weeds by jealous husbands fearful of their chastity. But there are no fixed rules except one—every woman makes the disguise work to her advantage.

Putting on men's clothes—the ultimate form of power-dressing—is the outward signifier of a certain shift in the heroine's values and perceptions. And so, having experienced both ways of life, she is free to make her choice. When the heroine discards her veils, gowns, and jewels, she throws away bondage. Men's clothes symbolize her liberation. And we all know the sacrifices a woman has to make while the spotlight remains on her, waiting for her to betray her femaleness in a man's world.

Immediately and satisfyingly, fairy tales redress this imbalance. Here, dressed as men, women break unthwarted through cordons of male power and rise to enormous heights—like the blacksmith's daughter they even succeed where men have failed. The skills of the lawyer, the physician, the knight, are all proven to be well within their grasp—sometimes they even become king. But in order to raid the vast stretches of their unexplored, disused inner female landscape and prove the potential that *they* know exists, they have first to put on men's clothes. And in britches, they can act out the qualities that go with the clothes—daredevilry, candid sexual expression and independence. And though part of the rhetoric of the fairy tale, the princess is by no means alone in this: peasant women, daughters of priests, wives of tailors, shoemakers, and doctors, all don the britches when the motivation is strong enough.

I noticed that with few exceptions there is a process at work in the cross-dresser's tale. She responds to a need or a call; she transforms herself swiftly and completely (often secretly too) in order to fulfill that need; finally, when her mission is complete she exposes her disguise to those who are significant and returns to her former normality. But the process intrinsically alters a vital dynamic in her life.

A woman in the guise of a man is the ultimate symbol of deception or metamorphosis, and since fairy tales, located in the realms of the improbable, have always been an ideal medium for allusion to the subversive, she facilitates manageable, sometimes hilarious reference to subjects that are generally taboo. Homoeroticism is one example—women fall in love with women dressed as men, women disguised as men fall in love with other women, men fall in love with women despite knowing them as men. But the linear and fixed sequence of the traditional fairy tale provocatively poses the question and moves on without inquiry. If the reader decides to pursue the point, then the tale has achieved one of its many aims—the stimulation of the mind beyond its existing framework.

Without a doubt there are problems inherent in the transformation. Men, conditioned over centuries, appropriate space in a different way. Perhaps, being attuned to a concept of "outside," they try to conquer it by flinging their arms over it and their legs around it and using it to surround their bodies like a protective and enlarging nimbus. Women on the other hand adapt to the confinement of "inside," tending to gather themselves in, squeeze the space out as they cross their knees, one leg lying directly over the other, arms held close to their bodies. Men and women sound and look different, they respond differently. We feel we can tell them apart despite their clothing. We talk of manly women and womanly men. But fairy tales, contrary to common currency, do not stereotype. Like dreams, they symbolize qualities and potential. They allow a great deal of leeway—child heroines fall in love and get married, for instance, without any indication of time passing. We may rationalize that once upon a time it was not unusual for girls to marry before reaching womanhood; in days of old, men often had long hair; the clothes of Eastern men and women were hardly different apart from the veil and the turban. Even so, since the heroine constantly places herself in situations where she may be exposed, sustaining the disguise is subject to enormous dangers.

Treachery, fraud, and immorality could in the currency of "once upon a time" have been punished with incarceration or even death. I was appalled to find in Deuteronomy wedged between a verse exhorting a man to help his brother nurse his fainting oxen and another one admonishing him to leave baby birds alone in their nests, the following injunction which became the basis of cruel sentences against cross-dressers: "The woman shall not wear that which pertaineth unto a man, neither shall a man put on a woman's garment: for all that do so are an abomination unto the Lord thy God" (Deuteronomy, 22:5).

The purpose of myth and fairy tale, in primal societies and early civilizations, was while entertaining, to prepare the listener for what might lie in store in real life. At some levels it remains so. Stories from the vast body of folklore available throughout the world demonstrate that life is a series of quests overcome by a combination of dogged determination, boldness, risk, and inexplicable bursts of luck. It is unpredictable because it has no obvious logic. Myth and story also teach that survival is negotiated in a number of ways: by trickery or honesty, industry or laziness, meekness or defiance, activity or passivity—the balance of opposites. Each situation is assessed on its unique merits—the heroine of one tale may reenact the behavior of a villainess of another. Fairy tales come from the land where disobedience can pay, idleness can bring rich rewards, and deceit result in honor. In short, it is the promised land—the land where nothing is impossible and judgment, if it arrives at all, can be astonishingly gratifying. The female cross-dresser embodies the successful conjunction of opposites.

In the subcontinent of India and Pakistan, where I was brought up—and particularly in my own family—storytelling was a positive activity. European fairy-tale classics, the Brothers Grimm, Hans Christian Andersen, and the Andrew Lang books, shared shelf space with Oriental tomes—the *Epic of Amir Hamza*, *The Chronicles of Azaad*—and bridging the gap was Burton's translation of *A Thousand and One Arabian Nights*. Stories were everywhere, from Classic Comics to encyclopaedias of Greek, Roman, and Egyptian mythology. I remember vividly the multiple role of stories, fables, and proverbs meted out as rewards and punishments or used to pass time together much like playing cards or board games. They were vital and powerful, communicating living attitudes, desirable outcomes, religious expressions, and moral perspectives. Women who dressed as men therefore expressed a valid female fantasy—breaking away from the bondage of gender. For a woman, putting away her female garb was as much about putting away the persona that came with it. And the change descended deeper, into her personality and her soul, bringing to the surface the magic of artifice and imagination.

I am delighted to confess that I remain enchanted with the heartiness of the heroines—their bold and blunt assumption of the right to self-expression, their determination to have their cake and eat it too, their reappropriation of the right to change roles out of womanhood and back again. As a child I never sensed a feeling of disapproval from anyone around. There was nothing in the broad shape of the tale that needed censoring. The anchoring of the tale in the lands of faraway, in times to which the clock cannot be turned back, was sufficient to contain the threat of subversion while at the same time providing the inexhaustible and magical potential for self-fulfillment.

The obviously uplifting effect of the cross-dresser's tale comes from two vital factors: the heroine receives unconditional recognition for her achievements after which her lifestyle becomes a *matter of choice*. This transforms her status subtly, powerfully, and irrevocably.

Transformation lies at the heart of the fairy tale and the cross-dresser epitomizes this process. Often, as in the narrative of the night watchman, the more crucial, inner transformation is overlaid by the concrete, outer change. But it is the internal reversal brought about by the heroine's experience that ultimately creates a new dynamic in the "old" situation; a browbeaten wife, though still performing the same duties, no longer feels put upon, and the daughter who has had her father released from the dungeon returns to the women's quarters with a new appreciation of her role.

In my versions of the stories I decided to try in some way to articulate the internal processes of the metamorphosis from dependence to independence. There was never any doubt in my mind that the heroines for my collection would come from legend and tale, but as I wrote I found that often I was serving my muse more than my discipline. As a folklorist I felt impelled to preserve the structure and content of the tales as I had first heard or read them. As a writer I wanted to leave myself free to develop the characters beyond their mere function, examine their motives, ponder on their problems, exult in their resolution. But fairy tales are more like memories than fiction, perhaps even like distant history. They existed before I put pen to paper and I found myself negotiating with them as one might, in fictionalizing the life of a famous person, negotiate with the truth, alter chronology slightly, highlight aspects of the subject's life, underscore certain elements—hopefully without distorting the essence of the whole. Or as a therapist participating in situations where the unarticulated must be articulated, the unnameable named. Naming and then owning is the essence of integration, the good, the bad, and the dubious are all part of the whole, and the cross-dresser reflects the synthesis.

In some cases this has not meant much more than giving the heroine a name, while in others I have explored unnameable inclinations—homosexuality, abandonment, the gender battle—those questions that felt so peripheral to a child of ten. I have tried to draw out the tone implicit in the situations of the tale—they are bawdy, ironic, serious, riotous. The purist in me is comforted by the knowledge that beneath the details, the plot remains unarguably the same.

I have written these stories in the spirit of the storyteller, resisting the temptation to bring a literary or historical authenticity to the tales beyond my own cultural experience. Like a storyteller, I have indulged my instinct to flesh out the personalities of the main protagonists, to stop along the way for reflection, to allow the peripheral characters to develop and to explore the unanswered questions that were raised in my mind as an adult and as a child, thrilled and entertained by the daring and the autonomy of women who wear the britches.

Shahrukh Husain,
London 1995

Handsome Heroines

A RIDDLE

FOR A KING

Vasily Vasilyevich? Vasilisa Vasilyevna? Is it a woman? Is it a man? The priest's daughter? The priest's son? King Barakat was in a quandary. So perplexed was he that he even visited the palace backyard to ask the advice of the old hag who lived there. And that was how Vasilisa's servant knew about his confusion and his curiosity.

Vasilisa Vasilyevna slapped her thigh and laughed.

"So the king wants to know if I'm a woman. I wonder why he's so concerned?"

"Well," replied the servant, "it isn't really any wonder at all, I suppose. Where was it you said he came across you?"

"I came across him," Vasilisa corrected her servant. "I was hunting in the woods; so was he. I had a sackful of game hung up behind me on the back of my gray mare—you know, the one with the gray mane—when along came the king with a very reasonable catch. I saluted him from a distance and rode on.''

"Well," completed the servant for Vasilisa, "it isn't a wonder at all, then. You rode off without stopping to greet the king as others would, so he became curious and asked his groom, 'Who's that young man?' and the groom replied, 'Not a man, sire, but a woman—the priest's daughter—Vasilisa Vasilyevna.' Well, at the very same time another attendant was saying, 'That's the fine hunter Vasily Vasilyevich.' So the king was confused.''

Vasilisa let out a loud laugh.

"Who's that man, eh? Not surprising, I suppose, not from that distance and with me in my hunting clothes. Well, he's not the first, I suppose, nor will he be the last. It's a puzzle to many. Am I a man? Am I a woman? If a woman, why do I wear britches? Everyone wants an answer. Well, you know, I never even thought about it myself!''

She stood up, knocking back her measure of vodka, hissed sharply as it hit the back of her throat, and drew her lips back over her teeth. She loved that hot feeling of the drink as it chased down her gullet and spread into her chest. She could drink with the best of them, could Vasilisa Vasilyevna, though her father, the gentle priest Vasily, was always telling her that drinking vodka was not becoming to a woman.

"I suppose we'll be hearing more from the king. Though what he thinks the old hag can tell him, I'm not sure, except a whole lot of superstitious mumbo-jumbo.''

She chuckled to herself as she stood up, smoothing down her trousers. Her father liked to see her neat and tidy, and she herself was fastidious about how she looked. She wandered into old Vasily's study, still chuckling. He would enjoy the story, she was sure.

She entered, as usual without knocking, to see the priest reading a letter—and look! it is stamped with the royal crest.

"Is that a letter from the king?" inquired Vasilisa, not sounding surprised at all.

"How did you know?" responded her father, amazed.

"Well, Father, let's just say I was expecting to hear from him."

Old Vasily shook his head, but he couldn't keep the smile from his lips.

"Daughter, daughter," he declared, "I don't dare ask you the reason behind this expectation."

"Well, Father, that's a pity," Vasilisa chuckled, "because I came here to tell you."

"Then tell me," said the priest resignedly.

So Vasilisa told her father about her encounter, then took the letter from him and read it.

"*Venerable priest Vasily,*" wrote King Barakat, "*I would like you to permit your son Vasily Vasilyevich to attend me in my palace and break bread with me at the royal table.*"

Vasilisa laughed aloud.

"So is this because he wishes to dine with a woman?" asked the priest astutely. "Or a good hunter like himself?"

"I'm a good hunter, whether you call me a man or a woman. But Barakat wants me to eat with him precisely because he doesn't know. Am I a man? Am I a woman? Am I the son of the priest? Or his daughter? Poor King Barakat! He's so desperate, he's asking old crones for advice now. And yet it's women they malign for their idle curiosity."

Vasilisa Vasilyevna? Vasily Vasilyevich? Man or woman?

Priest's daughter or priest's son? Vasilisa could barely keep the grin from her face when Barakat greeted her courteously, his suspicions superbly concealed. Vasilisa bowed low, made the sign of the cross, and raised her hands in prayer as she entered, and the king was gratified at her formal and correct greeting. In fact, he was so hospitable and so charming throughout the evening that Vasilisa felt a tiny twinge of guilt at her deception—though not for long. Barakat, after all, was hoping to dupe her too, pretending he was not confused or concerned about her sex. She waited, alert, for him to spring the trap he had laid for her on the advice of the old woman. But she encountered none and the evening came amicably to an end.

Finally, the king walked Vasilisa to the hall, thanking her for her presence and saying how much he had enjoyed the evening. And as she returned his thanks and his compliments, her eye fell on a tapestry hanging on the wall beside a display of rifles, swords, and other weapons. A strange rustic piece that you might find in the house of a peasant, bright and flamboyant, the elements within it vying with each other, garish colors against exquisite embroidery, refined thoughts against coarse exposition. The tapestry was remarkable by virtue of being on a wall amid a collection of armaments, and because the vodka had relaxed Vasilisa, she spoke without restraint.

"How strange to hang a tapestry among your swords, King Barakat," she remarked. "And not one I would expect to find in a palace! You'll find no such frivolous, girlish fripperies in my father's house. We wouldn't tolerate them, Father nor I."

And before the king could speak, Vasilisa Vasilyevna slipped away.

· ·

"The king visited the old hag again," reported her servant, now turned spy. "He said her plan had failed."

"What plan?" demanded Vasilisa.

"Well, it would seem that the old woman told the king to hang a tapestry on the wall. 'If she's a woman,' she claimed, 'she'll notice it right away; if she's not, she'll notice the rifles.' So that's what the king did, but the plan failed."

"So it did," roared Vasilisa, her eyes streaming with jollity. "I barely mentioned the guns and I did speak about the tapestry, if only to ridicule it. Poor King Barakat."

Well, it was not quite one week before the king sent another invitation to Vasilisa. This time, too, it was sent in the proper manner, to her father, seeking his permission to entertain Vasily Vasilyevich to dinner. Once again Vasilisa saddled her gray mare, swung herself astride the faithful creature, and made her way to the palace. And once again she could barely conceal her mirth at the memory of the king's frustration. All evening she remained alert for a trap. She enjoyed the king's conversation and his company, but this time the food was not so good as before. Every time she took a mouthful, hard pieces ground against her teeth in an unpleasant manner. At first Vasilisa was polite, surreptitiously spitting the pieces into her hand and flinging them under the table. Eventually she scooped the food onto her spoon, examining it with a sidelong glance as she spoke to the king to distract his attention. The offending pieces were round and glistened.

"Pearls!" she realized in amazement. "He's had the food filled with pearls! What a terrible waste."

By this time King Barakat's pleasant company and his hospitality and vodka had loosened Vasilisa's tongue and she complained aloud to him.

"Do they put pearls in your kasha, King Barakat? They could break a body's teeth! My father and I would not endure such girlish indulgence in our house, you can be assured. But I thank you for your hospitality all the same."

And Vasilisa Vasilyevna swept out of the palace before the king could open his mouth to respond.

Once again Vasilisa left King Barakat in a state of confusion. Once again he went to the old hag and once again it was reported to Vasilisa that the king was quite despondent about his failure to ascertain whether she was a man or a woman. Of course it was the old crone who had ordered the pearls to be put in the kasha.

"A woman will know they are pearls and store them in a corner to take home," she assured the king. "A man will think they are stones and fling them under the table."

The king was unconvinced.

"He cast them under the table, didn't he?" grumbled the old hag. "That means he's a man."

"He may have thrown them under the table," argued the king, "but he knew they were pearls. So we have achieved nothing at all."

Well, the third invitation arrived. Again it was addressed to the priest, again it invited Vasily Vasilyevich to break bread with the king, and again Vasilisa Vasilyevna mounted her gray mare and rode over to the palace. By now, though, she was beginning to wonder how long before her amusement turned to boredom, then irritation. Still, for now she looked forward to seeing the king and to meeting the challenges he set for her. He was a generous host and an entertaining companion and time passed pleasantly with him. And oh! how Vasilisa Vasilyevna enjoyed a challenge. The subtle and complex contests of the mind were so much more thrilling than the parry and thrust of a fencing blade. And King Barakat was a worthy partner, delicate in his ability to draw her into conversation, beguile her thoughts, and amuse her. Yet never once did he let her see he had anything on his mind other than to enjoy her company. The company of the priest's son, Vasily Vasilyevich. His jokes were just that bit risqué—never enough to overstep the mark; his questions just that bit leading—never enough to betray he was investigating, sizing up, testing the waters. He was a wily one, was King Barakat, and quite right, too, for a king to have those qualities. Vasilisa Vasilyevna found him a worthy opponent, and it reassured her to think he had honed those skills not across the table with a single guest but in consequential halls and courts with ministers and kings over matters of state, of life and death, war and peace. No, there was no doubt Barakat was astute and artful and as determined as any animal that ever lived.

So that night, as Vasilisa entered the now-familiar hall of the king, she looked around her carefully as she offered her customary prayer for king and country and crossed herself and bowed to east and west and north and south. Was there anything new on the walls? Anything unusual about the place? Anything she should be wary of? Nothing—or at least nothing she could immediately identify.

She straightened up and followed the king into the dining hall. As usual, Barakat plied her with food and vodka and they discussed the best methods of marksmanship and boasted of their respective achievements in hunting and arguing and riddling. And they slapped their thighs and knocked back little glasses of vodka down their throat in one throw and enjoyed themselves heartily. And Vasilisa wondered, "Has the king decided to give up his investigation? Does he enjoy my company so much that he has ceased to care?"

But Barakat's next words reminded Vasilisa that the crafty king was doing his job so well, he had succeeded in diverting her.

"Vasily Vasilyevich, we have been friends for some time now. And we have eaten together on several occasions—and told each other many secrets. So I do not think it would be out of place to ask if you would like to share a bath with me tonight. It is drawn and heated and if you would like to join me in the royal bathhouse, I should be delighted. Then we can enjoy each other's company awhile longer."

Vasilisa's face broke into an enormous grin of pleasure.

"Why, King Barakat. What a privilege! It is a long time since my last bath, and what is more enticing than a hot bath with plenty of water? After all, steam is to the skin what rain is to the hardened earth." She bowed deeply. "I should be honored to accept."

Well, Barakat was in the seventh heaven of delight. Now he would be bound to discover the truth. He embraced Vasilisa and led her immediately to the bathhouse, where an attendant entered to help him disrobe. In the next room, Vasilisa quickly undressed and slipped into the bath, luxuriating in the warm water a few moments before calling out to the king.

"Are you ready yet, Your Majesty? The water is hot and steaming."

"I'm ready but for my vest, leggings, and boots, Vasily Vasilyevich," replied the king. "I will not be long now."

So Vasilisa rubbed the skin of her body with soap and loofahs before calling out again.

"How long more, sire? I'm afraid the steam will begin to thin in the winter atmosphere."

"All but my boots and my leggings, Vasily Vasilyevich," the king responded. "I will be with you very soon."

So Vasilisa smoothed the soap off her body and rubbed it down with perfumed oils and called out a third time.

"Surely you've done with your boots and leggings by now, Your Majesty?"

And the king replied, "My leggings are coming off as I speak, Vasily Vasilyevich. I'll be with you presently."

Then Vasilisa emerged from the bath and, leaving the implements and soaps and perfumes neatly lined on the side, dressed herself and slipped away.

Outside, she mounted her gray mare, wrote swiftly on a piece of paper, and handed it to her servant.

"Give this to the king," she commanded, her voice shaking with laughter.

"You're a wily old raven, King Barakat," the message read, *"but you could not get the better of the falcon in flight. It has never been my intention to create a mystery. I would have told you that I am Vasilisa Vasilyevna and not Vasily Vasilyevich. You had only to ask me."*

ACROSS THE
SUNLIT COURTYARD

This story begins with a story which, it seemed to our hero the handsome cavalier Master Ambrosio del Andriami of Milan, came out of the mouths of everyone around him. And it had assailed Ambrosio from every direction since his arrival in Naples. It was a story, a local rumor, or a bit of gossip or conjecture, you could say. It was about "Nola," the most beautiful woman in Naples—perhaps even all Italy. Ambrosio was beginning to think he would never get anywhere near the truth because "Nola" (this was not her real name; no one knew her real name, so she was called by the name of the city from which she had come) was indescribable. Besides, no one had ever seen her properly and so imaginations ran riot. One man swore he had seen her all pink and rosy and plump and generous with golden hair pouring in kinked rivulets down her back and around her shoulders, a luscious water-flower blooming in a sun-filled river of gold. Another paid tribute to a severe beauty, pale as a lily, huge eyes dark as guilt, deep as penitence, hair black as sin and pulled austerely off her face emphasizing her exquisite bones, her finely chiseled nose, her elegantly modeled mouth. She was a creation worthy of a master sculptor, from alabaster skin to passionless limbs—for she was ungiving of herself. She was that model of morality, that container of virtue, that example of chastity that made all men despair.

Ambrosio del Andriami of Milan hated all the words that clustered around the concept of chastity. He turned away from that version of the rumor and wished he could dodge all accounts of Nola. But they came at him from everywhere. From here, from there, from out of the air, like flowers snatched by a conjurer, from the mouths of men, like multicolored ribbons making empty offers of delectation. Chaste she could not be; if she was, why was her husband so fiercely protective, so clingingly jealous? No, he comforted himself, she must have given him cause in the past. You could judge others only by using yourself as the yardstick, he always said, and he could think of no situation other than infidelity, or the tendency toward it, proven and demonstrated, that would make a man lock up his wife and keep her out of sight. And this man, her husband, was so jealous of her that he had risked the anger of the Duke of Calabria himself, who had tried in many ways—always unsuccessfully—to gain proof of Nola's beauty. Nobody knew for sure, or, in view of the duke's experience, would ever know for sure what Nola really looked like. The duke's spies had discovered, you see, that when Nola's husband went out, she went with him—dressed as a man. And since there were usually one or two other men with them, who knew which one she was?

Ambrosio took heart from the likelihood that Nola liked a bit of extramarital fun and, given the chance, would indulge herself quite happily. He took to hanging around across the street from the modest home of her husband.

JOANNI TORNESI, SHOEMAKER TO CAVALIERS boasted the sign outside his shop. Above, the windows of the residence were always dark, curtains drawn, and Tornesi was always in his shop.

"If only the wretch would go out sometimes," fretted Ambrosio.

"It's unlikely he will," responded his friend Tommaso Caracciolo. He had a truculent air about him, but Ambrosio knew it was just his way. "In fact, we know he doesn't, don't we?"

"Do we?" responded Ambrosio dully.

"That's what they all say."

"How much do we believe of what they say?" demanded Ambrosio. "That she's golden-haired and black-haired at once and that she's rosy as an apple or as white as snow at one and the same time and oversexed and undersexed with one and the same body?"

Tommaso shook his head. His friend was in a hopeless state.

"You've strumped women here and there and everywhere. Not a night went by without you having fun in some woman's bed—and you never looked back for any who wasn't hot on your trail. So why mope around for this one?"

He looked at Ambrosio, gaunt, haunted, eyes dull except

when they thought they sighted Nola at a window, skin lackluster.

"She's hardly going to love you when you look like that," he scoffed. "Get a hold of yourself, Ambrosio, and offer her something worth taking a risk for in the unlikely event that she ever gets a chance."

"If only he'd go out sometime. Just for half a day."

"You know he takes her with him when he goes out! That is one fact everyone agrees on." Tommaso was becoming angry with his friend. Lately Ambrosio seemed to hear what he wanted and become miraculously deaf to the things he did not want to hear. But he had to do something or Ambrosio would die or go mad.

"Go in and ask for some shoes," he told Ambrosio. "Sit by the inner door. It looks onto the courtyard and all the bedroom windows. He'll have his back to you and you'll have a perfect excuse for looking out to examine your purchase in the best light."

So Ambrosio took one faltering step forward to his destiny. He went into the shoe store of Joanni Tornesi, Shoemaker to Cavaliers. And he asked for this shoe and that shoe. Didn't the man have a finer leather, a more elegantly turned heel, a more interesting range of colors? Didn't he have a greater variety of styles? Something more original? Lighter? Darker? Springier? Firmer? Tighter? Looser? Buckled shoes? Bowed shoes? The demands continued. Joanni Tornesi, Shoemaker to Cavaliers, became quite dizzy and gave up hope of ever making a sale, but he couldn't risk losing a promising customer, a dandy by the look of him, and if Joanni pleased him enough, he'd probably keep coming back for more. He persevered. Time rolled on and Ambrosio del Andriami, noble and handsome cavalier, began to despair of the phantom woman ever appearing at a window. But he had to make sure he would be welcome back at this shoemaker's store. This man's possessiveness was legendary: if he guessed that the cavalier was in his store, sniffing for his wife, he would stop him coming back.

Ambrosio's poor head was running out of new demands and his heart of hope, and he decided he would let his eyes search the windows one last time.

"If she's not there," he vowed silently, "I will leave this shop, go back to Milan, and never think of her again."

He felt stronger once he had made that decision. He stood up, slipped his foot into a shoe, twirled elegantly, took it off, replaced his own, lifted the one he had just tried, and moved over to the window, where he looked at it against the light and passed it toward the window.

Red. Glowing, titian, burnished red filled his eyes, as it did sometimes when he laid finger and thumb across the bridge of his nose and pressed down his eyelids against the sun. A dazzling, burning red—the blood of his own eyelids, he had always thought. But he saw it across the sunlit courtyard now, gleaming against the invisible pane of glass.

And what else did he see? For his heart stopped as she raised her hand, pointed to the place he had loitered and pined when he had come to find her before. She knew! She knew and she welcomed him! Then she sank back and his heart sank with her.

But here! She's back and raises a glass of wine, a different red—dark, like the blood of virginity—raises it to him, kisses it, and draws the curtains over the windows. He thinks if he's struck blind now, this minute, it will be no worse than the frothy ruffles of those curtains, lining upon lining, foaming across the pain, shutting out the red blaze of an untouched dawn.

"They look good in the natural light," he muttered, barely seeing the shoes. "Let me check them by the door."

The sale was made. And the cavalier, drunk with love, generous with possibility, praised and paid the shoemaker lavishly.

"I'll be back for more of your masterpieces, soon," he declared. "A different pair of shoes each day. So set your mind to it, Tornesi, master shoemaker, and consider your fortune made!"

Ambrosio turned back to see that Joanni Tornesi had closed the store.

"I exhausted him!" he quipped, reporting the event to Tommaso.

"But not as much as you'll exhaust his wife—and yourself, come to think of it," guffawed Tommaso raucously, heaving his great body up and down and grunting suggestively.

Ambrosio was offended. He could not endure such coarse thoughts about Nola. His precious, beautiful Nola.

"It's not like that for me," he murmured. He would court her and woo her and worship her and only when she was ready and willing and full of desire would he go to her bed.

It must have been love.

From that moment on, Ambrosio's eyes pictured Nola in many ways. Sometimes she was wild and he calmed her, at others she was unhappy and he cosseted her, yet others she was frightened that he would not find her as beautiful as they all said and he reassured her. He had never been susceptible to stories of her beauty; it was the mystery that had engaged him. But now that he had found her, it was she, the woman, he loved and not the legend or the mystery. He would have sworn that he would have loved her body and soul even if she had the face of a squirrel.

Weeks went by and he was sustained by the wave from the window, the toast through the glass pane. He thought differently about chastity. Now, it was a wonderful quality and he believed Nola possessed the very essence of it—saving herself for their meeting. He visited the shoe store every morning at ten, positioning himself so that he could be seen from the window. Their daily rendezvous across the sunlit courtyard were enriched in his mind and became significant episodes in their distant but nevertheless passionate subterranean relationship. Each dalliance became a treasured memory. He had bowed, she had inclined her head. He had smiled, she had thrown her hands over her face: each encounter across the hours and days of their romance was rich and fulfilling. And shoes, he developed such an insatiable appetite for, that he had to find new lodgings to accommodate them.

Joanni Tornesi, Shoemaker to Cavaliers, became a very happy man and grew richer and richer as friends of Ambrosio's began to patronize him and rivals of Ambrosio began to compete by buying two pairs of shoes a day and doubling the gratuities Ambrosio offered. But Ambrosio arrived home after every encounter with his heart stirred and full, his mind singing, his eyes shining, his fancy supplying the touches, the textures, the warmth that was contained in Nola's person. They were heavenly bodies, important in the order of the cosmos, revolving round each other to ensure that the world retained its correct balance. *They were meant for each other.*

Ambrosio hardly noticed that he was alienating Tommaso.

He wandered about with stars in his eyes, a bloom on his cheek, a song on his lips, driving all the young women in society and out of it (and their mothers) to the nearest shrine or spell maker or wise woman to pray for his love. But love he had none to give, except to the shoemaker's wife. And he was content to wait and watch for his chance and make tender overtures to her in his mind and continue to woo her and court her and lavish money on her in the full presence of her husband.

Then one day he heard of the Festival of Santa Caterina at Formello. It was an annual festival. Everyone from around went to it.

"I hope you'll find time to be my guide at the Festival of Santa Caterina at Formello," he said with a casual air as he bought his pair of shoes for the day. He had made sure not to be too demanding that day. "I assume you will be going?"

Tornesi seemed to hesitate and Ambrosio was quick to jump in.

"Ah, I see, signor, that you have other more important engagements there. I should not have embarrassed you by asking."

Tornesi bowed, fawning.

"Indeed not, my lord. I would be honored."

"Come now, Tornesi, you don't have to stand on ceremony with me. You know I'm not the sort to hold a grudge. In fact, I'm not even sure I shall go. After all, the event does not have the same significance for me. I'm a stranger in Naples—no connections, no roots, you know."

Tornesi looked worried. The furrow formed by the dark hairs between his eyebrows pleased Ambrosio.

"You, on the other hand, are very deeply rooted in the

local tradition," he continued cunningly. "It was wrong of me to embarrass you. I apologize."

"You have misunderstood, Signor Cavalier," protested Tornesi. "I was simply taken aback by the enormous honor. I could not have imagined that you would choose to have me be your guide, when—"

Ambrosio threw his arms around Tornesi in a dramatic gesture.

"I think of you as a friend, man, can't you see that?"

And without waiting for another word, he swept out of the shop, leaving a small sack of gold coins on the table. By the time he had wooed Nola from her husband's home, he would have compensated the man so well in gold and trade that he need feel no guilt at all. But then, the affair between him and Nola was ordained, all of it, so there was no room for guilt anyhow. He was simply the subject of his destiny. These matters took years and years—the blink of an eye for God, so wise people said, was the length of a century to humans. Ambrosio accepted that the Fates would grant his union with his beloved Nola at the time for which it was ordained. Not a moment sooner, not a moment later. And he must not rush or push or ram at it and upset the balance and the order of things. Otherwise he would certainly have been to Nola's bed not once but a hundred times by then.

How he spent his days in planning and preparing and dreaming, a spring in his step, a song in his heart! He searched out the inns and innkeepers to find the place best suited to his plan. He bought himself clothes and wigs and hats and feathers and shoes, shoes, and more shoes. And he amused himself fantasizing what her shoes would be like. And what would the rest of her body be clothed in? Britches, he knew, and what else? A cloak, no doubt, to cover her so that no one could detect which of Tornesi's companions was his wife. Surely it would be easy enough to guess from her voice. How would Tornesi contrive to conceal her hair—her glistening, titian-red swathes of tresses, tumbling, rebelling, pushing against their harness, whatever that might be? A huge hat? A monk's hood? A scholar's square? Ah! But he need not worry, he would know his love wherever he saw her. Whatever she wore. He knew her soul, he recognized her movements: the flick of a wrist, the turn of her neck, the curve of her smile. He would know Nola at once.

And he did. Standing there opposite the Castello Capuano, having waited the entire morning, he saw Tornesi arrive with two men, both much younger than himself.

"Students," he explained to Ambrosio by way of introduction. "This is my wife's younger brother, Giulio, a medical student, and this is a family friend, Orlando."

"Giulia," breathed Ambrosio, feeling himself float above the ground. "So that's her real name. Giulia. I should have guessed it."

He shook her hand firmly, and in return felt some pressure that matched the fleet look in her eye as he gazed at her.

Ambrosio felt that time had come to a standstill.

And that day with her was the height of his endurance and agony. Had he been tied to a stake in a flame with the devil on one side offering water and sweet Jesus on the other promising salvation, he could not have suffered so much. To have his beloved red ruby next to him, their garments sometimes touching, their bodies often and intentionally bumping, their eyes deliberately avoiding the glance of each other—to have her next to him at last was such sweet ecstasy. But to be denied the chance to grasp her hand and clasp her to his breast, or to bury his head in her welcoming lap, or even to whisper sweet words of love. Oh, that romantic cavalier died a hundred deaths and rose again like the phoenix from the savage impatience of his own desires.

By the time evening came, the muscles of his face and head were rigid, his shoulders hurt, and his body throbbed from the tension of being with her yet forced not to talk to her or look at her or smile at her. He began to snap at Tornesi and Orlando and complain of his exhaustion until the shoemaker became worried that he had somehow annoyed the cavalier and would lose the best patron he'd ever had.

"To my lodgings," Ambrosio said at last. "I'm weary of waiting"—and he looked soulfully at Giulia as he said the words. "I feel I will not last much longer if things continue as they have"—he was losing control, quick, save the situation, throw Tornesi off the scent—"today. I have felt a fever gripping me hard all day and I think I'm really quite ill now."

Joanni Tornesi looked relieved. It was not his fault, after all. The cavalier was simply ill.

"I and my companions will walk you to suitable lodgings, my lord," he offered, "then we'll be on the way to ours."

Well, they looked at one place and another and another and Ambrosio proved as fussy as he was in his selection of shoes. If the innkeeper had rooms, he detested the place, if he liked the place, there were no rooms, and so it went on until everyone else in the party grew as tired as he. At last they reached the inn that Tommaso had checked out and approved as being suitable for his purposes: the right staff, the right facilities (and lack of them because that was as important in a plan of this detail), and the right number of rooms saved.

"See, Tornesi," he boasted. "If you look hard enough and persevere in your standards, you get what you want."

"Yes, my lord," muttered Tornesi miserably. "Now I and my companions must continue on our way."

"Have you got lodgings planned?" inquired Ambrosio.

"No, my lord, but it won't take us long . . ."

"Nonsense, Tornesi. You and your friends must stay here with me."

Tornesi shifted around in his cloak. "That would be too forward, my lord."

"Nonsense, man, you'll be my guests."

"No, really, sir, I cannot . . . I must not impose."

"Don't I pay you enough for those shoes I buy every day, Tornesi?" snapped Ambrosio. He was enjoying the game, so close to his profoundly desired goal that the delaying of the climax had suddenly become intensely pleasurable.

"It's not that, sir."

"Then stay. And you shall be my guests." He turned with a flourish to the landlord. "Three rooms more, landlord. For my friends."

The landlord, a giant of a man, looked a little perplexed, then shrugged and shook his head. The games noblemen played were the unreadable pages of a Book of Mysteries. He'd been told to keep four rooms free and prepared and he'd been paid for them in advance; he didn't need to worry about the interchange between his patrons.

When they had all settled into their rooms, Ambrosio called loudly for the landlord.

"Dinner for four men, innkeeper," he ordered, "and a good meal because we are weary from traveling."

"I wasn't asked to prepare any food," said the landlord.

"Well, you're being asked now," snapped Ambrosio. "Enough meat and sauce for four people."

"Meat? Sauce? Where am I to find meat and sauce for four people on festival night? It's all been sold."

"Well, shouldn't you have thought to buy some for your patrons?"

"We don't provide meals so late at night," complained the innkeeper.

"Well, send out for it, then," insisted Ambrosio.

The giant thought for a moment, then scratched his head. "Well, there's the family joint," he said at last. "There's plenty of meat on that still. But it'll have to be just the meat. I've no sauce for it."

"No sauce? Can't you cook some sauce? Meat without sauce is coarse and unpalatable."

"The fires are out," grumbled the innkeeper. "I can't light them again just for a sauce."

"Then send out for it."

"I can go out for sauce, Master Cavalier," leered the innkeeper, "or I can stay and carve your meat and serve it up. If I'm to do both, you'll be waiting for it all night."

"Can't you see I'm ill!" Ambrosio shouted. "How do you expect a sick man, a stranger visiting Formello for the first time, to go out at midnight and know where to find sauce?"

"One of your party, then," retorted the landlord, noticing that the others had appeared from their rooms and that Tornesi was sending furious glances across the corridor to Giulio, the young medical student.

"They are my guests," protested Ambrosio, "I can't send them out."

The giant shrugged. "Suit yourself. It's meat without sauce if no one goes, meat with sauce if someone does. I'll go and start carving."

He yawned pointedly and a long moan escaped his throat at the same time.

"I can't eat meat without sauce," groaned Ambrosio, "but if I eat nothing I fear for my health." He turned hesitantly to Tornesi.

"I hate to impose on you, Tornesi, but would you be kind enough to fetch some sauce? You know the place better than I do. Or perhaps one of your companions . . . ?"

"No, no," Tornesi interrupted, "they don't know the place. I'll go."

He summoned the other two to his room, then emerged a few moments later wearing his coat and ready to leave. Poor fool, but he'd brought it on himself. If only he had left his wife at home, there would have been no need for this lengthy and elaborate charade. But then, where would be the delicious ecstasy of waiting, the elusive experience of love—real love, love of the body and mind and soul together, so different from a quick strumping under the quilt, feathers flying, time flying, himself flying, faster, faster, so that he could get off and get away without being caught? Sometimes he did not even recognize the matron whose feather quilt he'd ruffled, in the street or across a room the next day.

Still, he felt some sympathy for poor old Tornesi, about to embark on a long, dark, lonely journey into town in search of a jar of sauce. At the end of it he would return to find that his whole life would be a long, dark, lonely journey henceforth. But stop! Don't tempt the Fates. They listen and can become jealous!

Superstition! Out with it! Ambrosio had become horribly superstitious since this whole affair, that first ruby moment of seeing her across the sun-filled courtyard, glowing red in the windowpane. Perhaps he would abide by the rules of the superstitious just a few days longer. Until all was settled. Why take chances?

He saw Tornesi to the door, apologizing, expressing gratitude, making excuses, offering rewards, watching as he disappeared slowly down the end of the street. Then he turned, exhaustion gone, the spring back in his feet, wings on his heels as he flew up the stairs to knock on Orlando's door.

"I wonder, Master Orlando, if you would be willing to go to Salerno to buy us some oranges?" Having delivered his question, he hesitated delicately. "I am told that they will be beneficial for my fever but, as you know, I am too ill to go myself. And being a stranger to these parts, I am afraid to risk . . ."

Orlando looked bemused. "I should be happy to go, Signor Ambrosio," he stammered, "only I have promised Signor Tornesi to keep an eye on his charge, young Giulio. And since I've promised, he is relying on me not to leave the boy alone."

"If you would permit it," offered Ambrosio, suddenly shivering and shaking, "perhaps the medical student would come to my room and advise me on my health? Then we shall both be looked after and kept from danger."

Orlando hesitated a moment, then, seeing the water stream from Ambrosio's eyes and the pathetic sight of this flushed, trembling cavalier so gallant and impressive when they had first met, softened his heart. What could be the harm?

"Certainly, my lord," he smiled, "that would kill two birds with a single stone. I know how much Joanni Tornesi respects Your Honor. And Giulio will be looked after while I go to fetch the oranges."

He turned into the room. "Giulio! Giulio! Master Cavalier needs your expertise. Go and tend to him in his room."

Giulio arose, sprightly and unhesitant, his eyes bright, his cloak swinging.

"How he cherishes his learning!" exclaimed Orlando. "How glad he is to put it to good use. Look, he's all lit up at the prospect."

Ambrosio resisted leaning over to look and made his way resolutely to his room, where in a moment or two he heard a knock. He leaped up to answer it, his plans about this moment's greeting fleeing his mind, his carefully thought out words disappearing, the painstakingly selected couplets and quatrains, sonnets and lyrics evaporating into a euphoric mist.

And there she stood, cloaked in the voluminous guise of manhood. Before he realized what he was doing he had pulled her into the room and bolted the door behind her.

"Your hair," he cried, fumbling wildly with her hat, "where is it, how could you have hidden it?" and it tumbled down, tendril after tendril, wave upon wave, settling on his arm like shimmering flames upon a branch.

"My God," he breathed, "but you're beautiful. More beautiful than anything anyone could describe."

Her eyes were green as they stared up at his.

"I had the advantage," she laughed, "I could see all of you." She took a step back from him and walked around him, pretending to take a critical look. "But you"—and here she draws her cloak more firmly around herself, covering and re-vealing herself in the same move—"you do not see me even now."

"It is the whole that I love," he gasped. "I don't need to see all the parts that form the whole."

"Well, Master Cavalier," she challenged, "what will you see first?"

"Oh, don't taunt me anymore," he smiled, coming toward her, arms outstretched. "Haven't we waited long enough?" And the next moment they were in each other's arms. Well then, words and caresses, looks and touches, dammed and held back for all those weeks, were suddenly flooding out. Their clothes came off as if they could no longer bear the heat and constraint of them and they marveled at each other. Neither, each swore, had seen the equal of the other before.

"You can't stay with him," whispered the cavalier, "you must come with me."

Giulia agreed. "I'm fed up with putting on these clothes," she pouted. "On our first day together we'll burn them on a ceremonial fire."

He laughed, asking, "What made him dress you this way?"

"Jealousy plain and simple," she answered. "He imagines other men's hands on my body and it chokes him and blinds him until he can neither bear to be with me nor without me. He hardly leaves the house and I'm locked up in it with his vile suspicions. When he does go anywhere, I must go with him. But he insists that as a woman out on a journey, I am vulnerable to all men."

She pulled on her cloak, inclined her head, and mimicked

in a deep, rasping voice, " 'It's for the sake of your chastity, my dear,' he insists. 'My chastity!' I say, 'I'm quite capable of seeing to my own chastity. You don't worry your head about it.' But not a chance. His jealousy chokes me and stifles me as much as it does him."

"Let's leave tonight," begged Ambrosio. "We may never get the chance again."

She smiled agreement and raised her mouth to his. Ah, what a rich cup of that ancient elixir called "love." They drank deeply and fell upon each other, intoxicated. More fumbling and humping, and in walks Master Orlando, bag of oranges in hand. He sees a mass, like an octopus, limbs and arms flailing frenetically, faster, faster in desperate frenzy. *They're making the beast with two backs.* He shuts the door, with himself inside. Then he opens it and shuts it again with himself outside. Then, having reconsidered his position, he's back in again, his neck rigidly averted from the uninhibited couple, though he's aware of their movements slowing down and coming to an end.

They watch him, laughing as the sweat pours off his kindly, honest brow. He mops it and tries to think, but his mind is blank. Good heavens! What goings-on! Master Tornesi must have known about the cavalier's penchant and the boy's proclivity. That was why he had asked him not to let the fellow out of his sight while he was away. And he shook his head, remembering how he had overheard him admonishing the boy at the fair for his wandering eye, insisting they share a room at night, while the boy asked what people would think except that Joanni Tornesi, Shoemaker to Cavaliers, traveled without his wife because he was fond of young boys. In fact, Orlando had heard Giulio say, people were probably already talking about it.

And now here he was, the sweat pouring down his face, the bag of oranges growing heavier by the moment. What on earth would he say to Master Tornesi when he returned with the sauce for the meat? There'd be no dinner tonight for sure unless it was this erring couple all chopped into pieces and roasted!

"I went to buy your oranges," he chokes, "I was doing you a favor. And look what happens. And look what I'm landed with."

"A bag of oranges," they chime. They're of one mind already.

He lets the bag drop to the ground with a soggy thump. "Damn and blast the oranges. What am I to say to Master Tornesi? How am I to explain my foolishness and your, your . . ." He splutters, lost for words.

"You don't," they chorus. "You keep your mouth shut."

He's outraged. "I can't do that."

"Why not?"

"It's dishonest."

They shrug, and before he has a chance to answer, the game's up.

"What's going on here?" thunders Master Tornesi.

Giulia starts up. Ambrosio pulls her back, throws a covering over her.

"We'll get through this fine," he murmurs in her ear. "Now is as good as any other time. And I'm a cavalier, I prefer matters direct and open. Tornesi doesn't stand a chance."

By now Orlando's all water, sweat, tears, drooling explanations, and apologies. Oh, hell! Oh, why had the kindness of his heart misfired in this horrible way? Had he only known the boy's tendency . . . but how could he ever have guessed that the cavalier preferred young men?

"Young men!" roared Tornesi. "What young men? That's my wife, you asshole!"

Orlando squared his shoulders, bloating with indignation.

"No asshole, sir, but an honest man," he objected, "deceived by you as much as by these young people. I would have expected better from a man of your gray hair."

"Why didn't you do as you were told?" shrieked Tornesi, growing hysterical. "None of this would have happened if you'd followed my orders."

"Orders, sir?" squeaked Orlando, his eyebrows raised. "Am I a paid servant?"

"You agreed."

By now Giulia and Ambrosio were rolling around the bed in fits of laughter. Orlando, morally outraged, Tornesi beside himself with jealousy. A moment later the giant stood behind the two fighting men. His eye fell on the lovers in the bed, took in the medical student's clothes on the ground, the red hair cascading down her shoulders. He roared with laughter and called out to his wife. A nightcapped woman, plump and pink, clutching a huge ginger tom in her hands, suddenly stood beside him. The cat, objecting to the kerfuffle, added to the caterwauling.

Shouting, laughing; laughing, shouting. It went on like that for a while. Then Master Orlando decided he'd had enough. He marched right up to Tornesi, positioned his face one inch away from the older man's, eyeball to eyeball.

"Master Tornesi," he said severely, "you were wrong to force your wife to dress like a man. You were wrong, because it is an affront to her character and you were wrong because you should have known that these days it is much more difficult to guard over pretty boys than women."

Well, there was little left to say after that.

And as for the meal, the landlord insisted on serving it up though Tornesi was determined to go hungry from the inn immediately. Orlando joined the couple and wished them well, whether they stayed in Naples or went to Milan. The sauce and the oranges were appreciated and enjoyed by all. The landlord joined in with many familiar phrases, like "All the world loves a lover" and "The love of a woman brought down Troy" and "The world is well lost for love." He ended with the platitude "What's sauce for the goose is not sauce for the gander." And though everyone present understood how the maxim might be relevant to the situation, they were not entirely sure it held.

But no one really cared.

Secure, at Last

Open the door! Open the door! There comes Rinaldo! He's sure to have a message from my husband.''

Servia looked up. Her lady Zinevra's face was glowing, dewy pink.

"How do you know?" she ventured. "There is no knocking on the knocker, no one has pulled on the bell."

"Oh, Servia, Servia, don't you see the dust rising in the direction of our house?"

Servia rose, then shuffled over to the window.

"I see a cloud of dust and in it a horse and rider," she

conceded, peering out of the window, her eyes screwed up against dust and sun. "But I cannot make out who it is."

"Servia, your sight fails you," laughed Zinevra. "That is Rinaldo and look, don't you recognize his horse? It lives in the country stables."

The rider emerged from the cloud and disappeared from sight under the balcony before Servia's eyes could focus properly.

"He has brought news from my lord," enthused Zinevra.

"You're a seer now, are you?" grumbled Servia, but she ruffled her mistress's hair and tweaked her chin and Zinevra saw the corner of her old sunken lips twist into the trace of a smile. Under her dour exterior, Servia was as sweet as syrup, as soft and wholesome as steamed pudding.

Fabia the maid was already dashing to the door as the rapping traveled up to meet Zinevra on her way down the stairs. She was right. The visitor was Rinaldo. And she was right again. He did have a message for her from her husband.

"Coming to the front door like that," muttered Servia. "That's not where servants used to knock."

She suffered from the snobbery of servants who have worked for generations in rich homes. She still remembered how offended her grandmother had been when her father had sent her to work for a merchant. Their family, Grandmother boasted, had always worked for the nobility. Well, as far as Servia was concerned, these merchants had proved themselves equal to a hundred nobles and more. Their money might be only a generation or two old, but the blood in their veins was bluer than blue—if blood could be judged by human kindness. But it was judged by titles and rank, and that was that. The noble of heart were rarely noble of blood, and of course it worked the other way too. How often could a servant of royalty claim to share food from the platter served to her mistress? Well, Servia always had. Now Fabia, the new girl, was like a friend to Zinevra. Her good, good, lady. And if that meant Servia must overlook Zinevra's lapses of protocol, then so be it. Of course she would never have mentioned them to her grandmother or mother had they been alive.

"Servants," she repeated, shaking away the censorious thoughts jostling in her head. "Servants rapping on the front door."

"Hush, Servia, you old snob. It's okay. He's brought a message from Bernabo. A message from my lord."

Servia shook her head again. Not surprising really that Zinevra should become so excited at the thought of her husband's arrival. He was away so much and the girl never looked at another man. Oh, men were to be had. They were to be had in droves. There was no shortage of men. Servia had heard from visiting servants that their ladies were not always averse to a little taster of this man and a little snifter of that one. Of course it was only while their husbands were away. And of course they did not really regard these acts as unfaithful. Men were men and they could not resist offering their attentions and a woman occasionally had need of a man. And if the men kept making it clear they wished to be used, well then, why not use them? It would benefit both—keep the circulation going. And of course the returning husband would be the eternal beneficiary of his wife's secret adventures. So in a way—admittedly not the way you tell priests about, but in its own way—it was a service rendered by a faithful and devoted wife to her husband. And what, Servia wondered darkly, did the men get up to while on their travels? Whoring and strumping indiscriminately. Of course to hear their servants boast and laugh, you would think they considered it the normal thing to do, even the right thing to do. In moments like that, when the men became coarse, their mouths glistening with saliva, their eyes searching out the reactions of the women, Servia thanked God her mistress was not the kind to commit infidelity. She could not bear to think that men crammed into some vulgar tavern somewhere might boast of their exploits in Zinevra's bed. But thank God her old ears would never have to suffer that ignominy. Zinevra was as pure as driven snow.

And what does she do in those uncommonly long months when her husband is away? The maidservants of others well may ask, for Servia could tell them. What did she do? Well, for a start, she had perfected her aim. She could shoot with masterly accuracy whether it was an arrow, a bullet, or a stone. And Enrico, her falcon, was no idle bauble. He was a deathly hunter. And what was more, Zinevra had trained him herself. Her very own self.

"And who was her trainer?" they giggled as they asked. Vulgar filth. But Servia's mistress was wise and had forestalled that. It was old Master Barbini—infirm of body and venerated for so many years of dedicated celibacy in service of the Church that he had forgotten what his dong was used for other than pissing with, unclean, filthy thing—not in a physical sense, mind, for Servia knew Master Barbini to be a very fastidious man, but in a spiritual sense.

Why then, she was half man herself, said the maids. No bed games and all this untoward concentration on hunting and shooting—no wonder she was not inclined toward men. Servia smiled darkly: she could roust them on that one too.

"My mistress," she gloated, "can turn a seam with the best of them. And look how finely she plants her stitches—minute as seeds mixed with pollen. And see how she makes flowers grow on the linen? Each one fresh and alive and vivid as the ones in her garden." They wanted more proof of her feminine accomplishments? It was in her cooking, her ability to run her home, her beautiful singing voice, her spiritual devotion. And of course in the way she pleased her husband so well that he never looked at another woman in all those months and days abroad. How did she know? Well, she was not so shortsighted yet that she could not see Rinaldo fall silent when the other menservants were boasting about their masters' rambunctious exploits. And his face so crumpled, you would think he was ashamed instead of being proud. She knew—Bernabo was faithful to Zinevra. Rinaldo's silences shouted it loud and clear.

And here he was now, tantalizing Fabia with the note, holding it above her hand while she bobbed for it like a clown.

"Your mistress," he was saying, "I must put it in your mistress's hand."

"My mistress is your mistress," pouted Fabia. "Or else your master is not my master."

"That he's not!" chuckled Rinaldo, and Fabia covered her face prettily as Zinevra joined in his laughter and Rinaldo bowed deeply in greeting. Servia approved. At least the young man remembered his etiquette—even if protocol had been forgotten, changed, lost, whatever.

"Let me have the note." Zinevra held out her hand.

There was silence for several moments as she read. Yes, she could read and write like a priest, add and minus like a merchant. Zinevra looked up and turned around in the same second, halfway up the stairs as she called down: "Servia, Fabia, help me prepare for my journey. Bernabo is at the country house—just twenty miles from here—I must get to him as fast as I can. My poor darling is waiting."

"So she's a seer too, now," commented Servia, and her voice smiled even if her lips had lost the habit. The child could bring a smile to anyone's heart.

They packed. As always, Zinevra was organized and methodical and today, as usual, she sang as she worked. She sang a hymn of praise and gratitude, and when that was done she sang love songs from the books she read and finally she skipped about singing the merry dancing tunes of the countryside and encouraging Fabia to sing with her.

It did not take long to pack and then, while Zinevra bathed and Fabia helped her dress, Servia packed food for the journey along with some of Bernabo's favorite condiments and confectionery from the pantry, specially prepared and preserved by Zinevra during the appropriate season. Finally, Zinevra said farewell to Servia and Fabia. The coach was waiting and she noticed there was no coachman.

"I will be driving you myself, my lady." Rinaldo bowed deeply as he spoke.

"Why, Rinaldo," laughed the lady, "I had no idea you were a coachman now."

"A man must learn to be many things to his master," he said, and Zinevra thought she was deceived because there seemed to be a grimness about Rinaldo's remark that she had never noticed before. The man was generally charming and jovial and she could understand why her husband liked to keep him around.

"Perhaps," she thought, "poor Rinaldo is tired. The long trip from Paris, then a twenty-mile ride to Genoa with the message, now the twenty-mile journey back. No wonder he is tired."

Then, on an impulse she stepped out of the coach again.

"Saddle me my mare," she commanded a hovering groom. "It will be much quicker to ride. And bring Rinaldo a fresh horse."

She turned to Rinaldo.

"I hope you have the energy to ride fast," she said. "I want to be twenty miles from Genoa in the shortest time possible."

Rinaldo nodded, the grimness, Zinevra noticed, not diminished. But the trip would be shorter on horseback, and once he was there, Rinaldo would be grateful for her decision and she would persuade Bernabo to let him have a few days to recover.

It was a long journey by any account and they had been traveling awhile in the dark, when they came to a deserted spot. The trees grew tall around it and the scrub was thick underfoot. The horses neighed and whinnied and protested as Zinevra pushed on, hoping to come out speedily at the other end. But what—? There was no other end. She brought her horse up short, reining it in skillfully. This was a clustering killer of a grotto, cut off immediately behind the growth by a bottomless gorge. And in the distance the wolves howled, making the horses nervous and restive.

Zinevra tugged at her mare's bit, turning her around—and what did she see? A glint of steel—Rinaldo flashing a knife—surely not at her? No, faithful Rinaldo was simply keeping the knife ready in case they were attacked by animals—the four-legged kind and the two-legged ones—that abounded in places like these. Aaaoooha! Aaaoooha! She shuddered as the howling of the wolves grew louder, closer.

"Good man!" she said a little shakily. "Good Rinaldo. No wonder my husband likes to keep you near him."

But she could feel Rinaldo's breath on her. Rough. Rude.

"Rinaldo, what—?"

"I have to kill you," growled Rinaldo, his voice deep with fear.

"But why?"

She held off his wrist as he brought the knife toward her.

"I have to kill you," he repeated, and again, "I must kill you," as if it were a prayer he had to rehearse.

"Have I ever harmed you, Rinaldo?" Zinevra inquired, and there was a command in her voice which made his servant-nature hesitate and obey.

"You have not," he replied.

"Then why do you want to kill me?"

"Because I have been ordered to kill you."

Zinevra gasped. "Ordered? By whom?"

The man hung his head; his wrist went limp against the steely pressure of her hand.

"Who ordered you to kill me?" she insisted, and when she heard no answer, added, "No one. Is it for money, then?"

"No," he murmured unsteadily. "Your husband wants you dead."

Silence sang and teased and echoed in her ears like howling wolves. No, the sounds of this place, the deception of the dark, they had contorted the sounds of Rinaldo's voice. Or else the man was lying.

"No!" she shouted above the cacophony. "Tell me why you want to kill me."

"Because my master, your husband, instructed me to kill you. Why he wants you dead I don't know. It is not up to a servant to find out why his master gives him orders. It is not for me to reason why."

And in a flash he had gripped her by the arm. "Commend your soul to God," he ordered, gruff and growling again. "My master told me to show you no mercy."

"Wait," Zinevra commanded. "Have you no fear of God and the hereafter? Is your master going to save your soul from purgatory?"

The man hung his head.

"Here is a way to solve the problem," she continued without giving Rinaldo a chance to speak. "I will give you a set of my clothes. Stain them with blood and take them to your master. Tell him you have killed me and left me to the wolves."

The man opened his mouth, but Zinevra hurried on, not allowing him a moment to protest.

"Give me your clothes—I will go to sea and never be seen again in Italy so Bernabo won't know you let me go. Follow my plan and you will be safe. Here is some gold and my horse. May God have mercy on you."

Zinevra spoke forcefully and with a finality no servant could ignore. Besides, Rinaldo had only admiration and gratitude for Zinevra. He looked around in his saddlebag and found an old doublet and hood, which he gave her. Then he took her horse and left.

Aaaoooha! Aaaoooha! Aaaoooha! Aaaoooha! The cry of the wolves pursued Zinevra as she ran, shaking from her skirmish with death. But how she wished Rinaldo had been harder to persuade, because that would have indicated that it was he and not Bernabo who wanted to kill her. The money, she told herself, scrambling desperately for something else to convince her, Rinaldo took the money—that was what he wanted. He was lying about Bernabo—shielding himself behind his master. But no, she thought as she rested her head on a rough-hewn post, she had seen the hunted look on his face, the terror in his eye. He was acting under orders, not on impulse. She let her hand run up and down the jagged surface of the pole and followed the movement with her eye. There was a sign suspended from it that announced the name of the inn to which it belonged. But for Zinevra it was also another kind of sign—a sign to take hold of herself and her destiny. Fate had brought her here and she, running in her blind fear, had not even known when she arrived.

She went in and procured herself a room. The landlord's wife was a kindly soul and was happy to lend her a needle and some thread. That night Zinevra set to work cutting and altering the old doublet so that it fitted as if it had been sewn for her. She divided her chemise into several pieces and stitched it into hose. Then she cropped her hair short, dressed herself in her new clothes, and walked to the door to go out and buy herself a few provisions for her journey. She thrust back the heavy bolt into its iron casing and walked out a different person.

As Zinevra strode through the village, not a single person seemed to notice she was a woman.

"Good-bye Zinevra," she thought, "good-bye forever. In your incarnation I lived a good life. But now I'm born again. And this time I will live for myself."

The next morning, after a good night's rest, as she made

her way to the coast Zinevra thought a great deal about the way her last life had ended and the second begun.

"In a way Rinaldo will not be lying when he tells Bernabo he has killed Zinevra. Bernabo's wife is dead. Faithful Zinevra, sitting at home, waiting, waiting for her husband's pleasure, housebound Zinevra is dead. But many of her skills and accomplishments and experiences will still be useful to me."

When she thought about it, she realized that Zinevra had never really had many choices except to be a good wife or not to be a good wife. Well, her virtue had not earned her anything in the end. In this new life though, she had many choices. She could choose almost anything—fate was wide open to her—anything, that is, except to be a wife.

"For a start," she laughed, "I can choose my sex. I will be a man so that no one suspects who I really am. Zinevra is the wife of a famous merchant and his associates travel far and wide. I can choose my own name—it will be Sicurano da Finale."

Sicurano da Finale, a young man with cropped hair and an assured manner, was seen at the coast within the week. He asked questions—so many questions that some captains became impatient and others suspicious. But most just answered his questions. And they all knew he was not your ordinary cabin boy. No shoe shiner and piss cleaner he, but clearly a wellborn young fellow who asked questions about the quality of the passengers, the merchandise to be carried by the ship, the ports at which it was likely to call, and the jobs available to a person with his qualities and training. It was clear he was educated, the captains agreed, but what his training was exactly they did not know.

Nor, somehow, did they dare to ask, because Sicurano handled them in such a manner that they felt obliged to please him with their answers. Then, having satisfied his questions, they had the sense that they were waiting for his approval or his praise, while he on the other hand withdrew from them as if he would weigh up their answers before granting them the privilege of employing him.

"Extraordinary!" commented an old sea dog as he heard the captains discussing the young man. "It is the boy who needs you. Yet you're acting as if he is the one with the favors to bestow."

"Have you heard him speak?" asked one, awe-stricken.

"Did you know he is capable as any merchant of accounting?"

"And reads and writes, and even cooks."

"And claims to have the skills of an experienced butler who has waited at the tables of the grandest men."

"Well then," grunted the old sea dog, "let him get a job that fits his skills. Clearly he knows nothing about seamanship. If he did, he would beg for a job at any cost and take the first one he got. The arrogant young whippersnapper! What is he looking for anyway? And you worthy seamen reduced by him to a bunch of quivering cabin boys. For shame! For shame!"

"What I'm looking for," said Zinevra when the captains crowded around her the next day, plying her with anxious questions, "is the ship that is going farthest away from the shores of Italy. And a captain who will take me with him on his trips inland and perhaps allow me to do some business for him and if destiny should present me with a good opportunity, be prepared to leave me behind."

A bulky man stepped forward. A Catalan by the name of

Encerarch, he had stopped in Alba to replenish the cargo of one of his fleet of ships before he set sail again to distant lands and the legendary wealth of the sultans of the Muslim empires.

"My carrack is sailing to North Africa," he said, "and if Signor Sicurano da Finale can convince me that he has business skills and will make me a penny rather than losing it, I will gladly let him conduct some of my business for me. As for the possibility of remaining abroad—I have sailed with many men in the course of thirty years or more and I have never yet met one who is indispensable. Particularly if he, or someone else, is prepared to make his release worth my while. And one thing I have learned in my work—the moment a man sets his mind to another job, he's no good anymore except in the one that's taken his fancy."

"Then one final condition," announced Sicurano, "and you shall be my master. I will serve you in any way I can— whether as a scribe or an accountant, a servant or a companion, a cook or a hunter—I will be any of these. But if you miss your wife, or the young lads you sport with in the side alleys when no one is looking—then you must find someone else. These activities are not part of my work and I will not put up with them. I make this condition publicly so that once you have given your word you cannot back down or you will have to answer to these good people."

The burly Encerarch turned a mottled shade of purple.

"Why, you cheeky little . . ." but his words trailed away as he saw a look of warning in Sicurano's eyes. If he did not agree to this young man's conditions, he would lose not merely the chance of enjoying the skills of many servants while paying for one, but suffer a certain humiliation before his peers. Be- cause though they all indulged in the same activities at sea, they rarely confessed to them. So instead of being angry, the man laughed and agreed in everyone's presence to Sicurano's conditions. A deal was struck and the next day they set sail for the continent of Africa and more specifically a country there by the name of Egypt in which was the ancient city of Alexandria.

Along the way Encerarch was well served by Sicurano, who proved to be a particular asset when it came to training the young falcons he hoped to use as bait for an audience with the Sultan of Egypt. Untrained, the youngsters were of great value; tamed and trained by Sicurano, they were invaluable! This service alone would prove so fruitful that it would pay many times over for Sicurano's employment, board, and keep. So it was no wonder that Encerarch made sure to bring his young assistant with him when he sought an audience with the emperor. Sicurano it was who would make the creatures fly and sit and attack and fetch and finally train the emperor and his men. And so pleased was the emperor with this young man, hunter by skill, nobleman by demeanor and deportment, scholar by wisdom and learning, he asked Encerarch to leave Sicurano with him. And in spite of everything the Catalan had said when employing the young man, he was reluctant to lose him.

"Do you want to stay in this remote country?" he asked Sicurano discouragingly. "Away from your home? Heaven knows when you will get the chance to return if you find the place doesn't suit you."

"Remoteness is only relative," retorted Sicurano. "Besides, home is too full of old memories for me to go back. No. I like Alexandria. I don't find it 'remote,' at least while I'm in it. I think I have a future here."

"An uncertain one for sure," growled the Catalan. "These sultan types are terribly unreliable. One day they love you enough to bestow lands and titles on you, the next they're having your eyes gouged out with red-hot pokers. And if you're unlucky enough to escape, you only prolong the agony. There's not a stone under which to hide yourself. They turn them all until they find you—then it's back to the red-hot pokers and dungeons. No, you'd better come with me. Who knows when another European ship will land here?"

"Sooner than you think," replied Sicurano confidently. "I hear there is a trade fair at Acre soon. People come from all over the world—Saracens and Christians—and if I find Alexandria does not suit me, I will return to Europe with one of them. But as for Italy—I will never go back to her shores."

At last Encerarch knew he could not dissuade Sicurano from staying in Egypt, and set sail, leaving the boy with the sultan, who, in appreciation of the young fellow's many talents, promoted him to higher and higher positions.

Not long afterward, the sultan began looking around for someone to begin preparations for the trade fair at Acre. Still wounded and mystified by Bernabo's actions, Sicurano volunteered. Italian merchants were intrepid travelers and never missed a chance to buy and sell in countries that promised to make them richer. It was likely that among the arrivals in Acre Sicurano would find a merchant who could shed some light on the enigma that still tortured her. What had made Bernabo hate her so much that he wanted to kill her?

"I know a little about trade and sales," Sicurano told the sultan when preparations began for the trade fair at Acre. "If Your Majesty wishes, I can help plan it."

The sultan decided immediately to appoint Sicurano.

"You can be governor," he said happily, "and if you are also captain of the guard, you can protect the merchants. Then they will be safe here and take back stories of the peace and plenty and hospitality of Egypt, by the grace of Allah, who is Great and Beneficent. You speak the language of my country well now, and I know you will be a good ambassador."

So it was that Sicurano da Finale came to be in Acre when the merchants assembled from all over the world. Among them, Sicurano saw, were many Italians—from Pisa and Genoa, Sicily and Venice—but Bernabo was not among them. Partly relieved, partly disappointed, Sicurano kept a wary eye out for him all the same and regularly toured the shops of Italian merchants. Then one day quite by chance she saw on display a girdle, a purse, and a few other trinkets. She pulled up her horse, dismounted, and examined the items at closer quarters.

"Yes," she said to herself, "it's as I thought. These are my things."

Sicurano assumed an air of nonchalance as she wandered over to an attendant.

"What is the price of these articles?" she asked. "And to whom do they belong?"

"I'll fetch my master, Your Honor," stammered the attendant, bemused to find the captain of the guard at his master's shop. "If Your Honor will wait here please, Your Honor."

The next moment a richly dressed young man appeared in the store.

"Welcome, welcome," he said, flattered by the presence and interest of the captain of the sultan's guard. "I am Ambrogiuolo da Piacenza and I am highly honored by your visit. I gather there is something in my humble shop that takes your fancy."

"These articles here." Sicurano pointed blandly to the girdle and purse.

"Why," Ambrogiuolo replied, laughing deviously, "they're not for sale. But if you've set your heart on them, you may have them free."

"He knows I'm a woman," Sicurano thought, seeing the merchant's conspiratorial smile. Panic choked her throat. But she squared her shoulders and spoke calmly.

"I see you find it amusing for a soldier to ask about a woman's things."

Ambrogiuolo laughed loudly. "Not so, sir, not so at all. I smile when I remember how I came by them."

"And how was that?" inquired Sicurano, sensing that the Venetian was about to give her a vital clue to Zinevra's death. "Unless, of course," she added cunningly, "it is confidential."

"It is no secret," laughed Ambrogiuolo. "In fact, by now the protagonists of the tale are quite infamous. You see, these things were given to me by a Genoese lady, Zinevra by name, the wife of a merchant by the name of Bernabo Lomellin. Lomellin and I spent a long time together on a journey once and I wagered that I could seduce his wife in his absence."

"And did you win the bet?" asked Sicurano, mesmerized.

"Why, of course I did," Ambrogiuolo boasted, "I see the captain has not had much time for women—no wonder he has achieved such status at so tender an age. How else do you suppose I came by the lady's personal possessions? She forced them on me, begged me to keep them near me to remind me of her. And so, here they are."

"Ill-gained trophies," murmured Sicurano as the destruction of Zinevra flashed before her eyes. Bernabo's vicious injunction, Rinaldo's attempt on her life. At last she knew why her husband had wanted to kill her. But whatever this man had told him, he should have spoken to her before condemning her.

"And you told Lomellin, I presume," she inquired. "You told him that you had cuckolded him?"

"Why, of course. And he paid me the grand and foolish sum of five hundred gold florins. Just as well, because I was traveling past Genoa not long afterward and word was that he had his wife killed. He made no secret of it, I gather, and ruined himself soon after."

Ambrogiuolo shook his head at Lomellin's folly, laughing, wiping away tears of mirth.

"The flesh of his belly wobbles when he laughs," noted Sicurano inconsequentially. "I wonder whether he ever spares a regret for the lives he ruined?"

She was numb from top to toe, from inside out. Her brain felt as if it were past thinking, except for one thing. She would not let this man get away without learning what it was like to have your life destroyed. How it was to lose everything including your very self. How terror fills you with humiliation and despair, and anguish becomes an indestructible part of you.

"It is now," she told herself, "that my true trial is beginning. I will force myself to put up with this man's odious company. I will listen to his lies about dishonoring me and causing my death." She swallowed hard. "I will pretend to enjoy his company and persuade him to return to Alexandria if necessary, until I find out enough to hang him with."

Once Sicurano's mind was made up, she never failed to achieve her goals. So it was that Ambrogiuolo, the vile Venetian, returned with her in all comfort to Alexandria. And withholding her secret like the great, riddling cat that watched over the desert, Sicurano pursued her end.

She tempted Ambrogiuolo with the promise of wealth

untold, with the possibility of titles and power and much more besides. And occasionally she would ask about Bernabo. What had actually become of him? Ambrogiuolo did not care enough to find out. Did Ambrogiuolo feel a little guilty perhaps? Enough to help the man get back on his feet? After all, it was Ambrogiuolo's deeds that had destroyed the man's marriage and resulted in such catastrophe. Eventually, worn down, Ambrogiuolo agreed, yes, perhaps he was a little to blame for Bernabo's ruin. But he had not known when he issued the wager how weak the man was. After all, other men accepted their wives' peccadilloes. It was human nature and as long as it did not dull the women's appetites for their husbands and they dealt discreetly with their amours, why, everyone was happy.

"Of course I understand it is not like that in your country," he explained hastily, seeing Sicurano's shocked expression, "but in Italy, things are very different."

Sicurano clenched her fists and set her teeth and bit back the words that came to her tongue. She was too close to her goal to spoil things now. And when she had cooled down a little, she asked pensively: "Why don't you invite Lomellin to Alexandria? You have seen for yourself how easy it is to make a fortune here. You can help him back onto his feet. A good deed never goes unrewarded.

"Besides," she added slyly, seeing Ambrogiuolo's hesitation, "the sultan is always impressed by generosity of spirit, and you can be sure I would let him know what you are doing."

So Ambrogiuolo extended an invitation to Bernabo through some Genoese merchants who, like him, had stayed behind to supplement their earnings from the fair. He would be his guest and the guest of his patron the governor and captain of the guard, who would help him reclaim the fortune that he had lost.

"And now," Sicurano told Ambrogiuolo, "I will introduce you to the sultan and you can tell him about your triumph with Zinevra and how today by inviting Bernabo Lomellin to Alexandria with the intention of making amends, you have proved that you are made of nobler stuff than you admit."

Puffed with self-importance, Ambrogiuolo da Piacenza told his story to the sultan with embellishments and flourishes and postscripts enough to keep the court laughing and the emperor amused and everyone agreeing wholeheartedly that a woman like Zinevra deserved the death her husband's servant had inflicted on her. But Bernabo Lomellin had, after all, been wronged. It was just and right that Ambrogiuolo should help him get over the distress caused by his wife's faithlessness and put him back on his feet.

Little pieces of Sicurano died as she heard the men speak with one tongue, and one heart behind it. Not a soul questioned Ambrogiuolo's story. Not one man asked how it was that Bernabo had so seriously misjudged his wife. Moreover when Sicurano tried to put forward these questions, the others laughed and teased her for her innocence. Women, they said, were frail and easily tempted whether they were in Europe or Africa or India. That was why they were kept in check by religion and society.

"Everywhere in the world is the same," lamented Sicurano to herself. But she held her peace. Bernabo would be here soon. Then she would somehow extrapolate the truth from Ambrogiuolo and at last there would be retribution for him and redress for Zinevra. But every day was a journey into the heart of a sandstorm, every night the weight of a mountain crushing the breath out of her as she lay alone until at last Bernabo arrived.

But what a Bernabo! How her heart bled to see him dressed in clothes of coarsely woven fabric! His shoulders stooped, thrusting out his neck like a heavily burdened tortoise and at the end of it a head drooped. He was grayer too. Not the tall, proud Bernabo she had sent to Paris confident in the knowledge that he would return as pure and loving and trusting as when he had left. No. This was not the husband she had sent away; a different man had returned in his place. It was not Bernabo Lomellin her husband who had ordered her death, but this warped man created by the scoundrel Ambrogiuolo to match his other invention—wanton Zinevra, who had not been able to get him quickly enough into her bed.

"Oh, Bernabo, Bernabo, would I have let you go at all to Paris if I'd known I would never see you again? Or would I have wrapped you up in my love and held you in my arms, safe and secure, until the next time?"

Sicurano turned away, blinked back her tears, warned Zinevra not to make an appearance. But Zinevra was as determined a person as she—and now, suddenly, she was reemerging, wanting to be part of this vindication Sicurano had planned for her. But no, Zinevra, not yet, please, not yet. Or all may be lost.

Sicurano da Finale went to the emperor that very day.

"Bernabo Lomellin has arrived," she said. "He is a broken man. I have arranged for him to stay with a merchant, a virtuous man, who will tell him about the business opportunities in this empire. Please summon Ambrogiuolo and Bernabo urgently and order Ambrogiuolo, on pain of death, to tell the truth about the Zinevra affair."

The sultan looked a little bewildered.

"Very well, my governor," he ventured, crinkling his brow, "but what exactly am I to expect? I thought Ambrogiuolo was your friend and that he was trying to redress the terrible sin of seducing his friend's wife."

"There is more to the story. I beseech Your Majesty to get the whole truth from Ambrogiuolo," replied Sicurano. "And punish him according to his sin."

The sultan raised a mighty eyebrow. "And you are sure there is a sin to punish?"

"I know there is," replied Sicurano simply.

"Well then, bring them both in," conceded the sultan, sensing that this favorite of his had a pain in his heart the size and texture of a craggy mountain, and that the exorcism of that pain consisted in getting to the bottom of Ambrogiuolo's sins.

The two men appeared before the sultan and all his courtiers.

"This," announced the sultan, "is a court of law. We are gathered here because my beloved governor wants me to solve a conundrum for once and for all. It is an old riddle involving the ancient triangle of love—the husband, the wife, and the lover. Two men and a woman, two women and a man—which is the worse? Well, we all know which is the worse.

"Man, we admit, has a tendency to roam. He looks for women when he is away from home, this is his nature. But a woman without her virtue is nothing. Lower than an animal. For it is in the body of the woman that our progeny is conceived and formed. How is a man to be sure that the product of her womb is his seed unless he is entirely sure she is virtuous?

"With these solemn thoughts let us open our case.

Bernabo Lomellin, we hear you ordered the death of your wife. Let us hear your cause and determine whether the execution was justified. All present will listen without interrupting and evaluate your words with care and attention."

At the sultan's invitation, Bernabo jerked forward as if someone had hit him. His face turned ashen and his brows drew so close together, they sketched a single line from one end of his forehead to the other.

"I did not know," he faltered, "that I was brought across the seas and deserts to tell my tale of shame and misery to the great sultan. But since it torments me and wounds me all the time, repeating it now will not make it any worse."

Bernabo lurched to the front of the spectators as if weakened by the prospect, and the sultan ordered him to be seated. He thanked the emperor, wiped the sweat from his brow, ran his fingers through his thick and unruly graying hair, and began, slowly, in a mumbling voice, to speak.

Bernabo's Tale

When merchants from one country are abroad in a strange land, they have a tendency to get together. And so it was that some important Italian businessmen in Paris met at a hostelry one night, at the end of a day's work. They ordered the best food and the finest wine and talked about their businesses and exchanged news of who had succeeded where and how much money they had made. As night drew in, they were all very relaxed in each other's company. They began to talk about their homes: which part of Italy they came from, where they lived, how much they missed it; when they would eventually be able to stop traveling and stay at home to enjoy the fruits of all their journeying and hard work. Most believed they would have to continue their travels until they had a son old enough to take over from them. Others had nephews, even trusted employees, being groomed for the job and they were waiting to be sure of a certain level of competence and loyalty before handing over responsibility. But there were those who did not want to stop traveling.

"I miss my wife, she is a wonderful woman," laughed one, "but oh, the joys of a passing flirtation, the pleasure of the chase, the thrill of conquest when both parties know the liaison must be fleeting—the sweetness of the pleasure that is like a one-time-only draft of nectar—with no conclusions and no consequences. It lingers like a fantasy and sustains you until the next unique experience."

"I agree," reflected another. "I have to admit I love my wife and I would never leave her for another woman. She is, after all, the mother of my children, the mistress of my home— but I could not give up other women, particularly when I am away from her for such long spells. Nor, I believe, would my wife expect it."

"Are you saying that you expect your wives to be faithful," asked Bernabo, astonished, "when you are not?"

"I cannot speak for my wife," laughed Sebastiani, "but for myself, I admit wholeheartedly, whenever a girl I fancy comes my way, I give the go-by to the love I bear my wife and enjoy the newcomer as best I can."

"So do I," chimed a number of others.

"Because," Giuseppe continued for his friend, "I know that my wife tries her fortune while I'm away—and so it's a question of 'do as you would be done by.' All's fair in such an instance, isn't it? The ass and the wall are quits. We remain faithful when we are together and there is only one rule to be observed. Never, never make any reference to lovers, she to yours or you to hers, or you will fall into the trap of suspicion and jealousy."

Most of those present—three out of five men—admitted to regular acts of infidelity. What was worse, they accepted that their wives were unfaithful and it bothered them not a jot. Bernabo Lomellin was incredulous.

"And you have no objection to your wives indulging in casual amours?" he inquired.

"Would you prefer them to have serious ones?" guffawed Giuseppe. "I wouldn't. There'd be far too much disgrace involved."

"Women are weak, we all recognize that," explained Sebastiani earnestly, slightly uncomfortable that Bernabo was taking the moral high ground. "Men are sexual animals, they need an outlet. It is a physical necessity. So women must be allowed the occasional weakness."

"I don't accept either," protested Bernabo. "Adultery is a sin for everyone. My wife is pure as the snow, as virginal as spring water."

"And," said Ambrogiuolo, the fourth man, provocatively, emerging from his silence, "is she ugly?"

"Ugly?" Bernabo smiled at the question. "She must be the most beautiful woman ever created. Fashioned, as the saying goes, by God's own hand. She is perfect."

"Foolish?" Ambrogiuolo asked aggressively. But his attempts to ruffle Bernabo seemed to miss their mark. Bernabo was like a drunken man, intoxicated by the wine of his wife's memory. Heady drink, it made him feel invulnerable, omnipotent.

"Quite the contrary. She is more intelligent than most men. I am blessed with a wife who is perhaps the most perfect paragon to be found in Italy. She has all the virtues proper for a lady. Even those of a knight or squire. She is beautiful, still quite young, handy, hardy, and clever beyond all women in embroidery and other women's handicrafts."

"Well then," concluded Ambrogiuolo, "I believe she must be arrogant and a show-off. Which, given her wisdom, leads her to cut herself off, in case she gives away too much about herself, which would make her vulnerable to jealousy and gossip."

"Not so," intoned Bernabo, desperately missing Zinevra and wishing he could hold her in his arms at that very moment and drink deeply from her ruby lips. And drink, in a manner, he did, because his voice was light, his thoughts dizzy as he continued. "Zinevra is well mannered, discreet, and sensible, and fit to wait at a lord's table as a squire or a manservant—the best and most adroit that could be found for love or money."

He held up his glass and stared into space, still speaking like someone in a hypnotic trance.

"She can manage a horse, fly a hawk, read, write, and cast up accounts better than any merchant. And I would wager my life that it is not possible to find a woman more honest or chaste than Zinevra. If I stayed away from home for ten years, the rest of my life even, Zinevra would never think of an amour with another man."

Ambrogiuolo laughed, a loud and ugly laugh.

"Is it by patent of the emperor that you were privileged to have a wife like that?" he leered.

"No," retorted Bernabo, beginning to get a little angry, "I think my good fortune has been conferred on me by God." Now he spoke dreamily again: "And you will agree, probably, that God is a good deal more powerful than the emperor."

Ambrogiuolo's expression turned indulgent.

"I've no doubt, Bernabo, that you believe what you say. But I fear you've been a careless observer of the nature of things. Otherwise you could not possibly talk so idiotically about your wife. And you are so ignorant of the whole business that you look down on us for speaking honestly and freely about our wives. You claim our wives are not as wonderful as yours, so I can't let the discussion drop. I believe that in all creation, man is the most noble, and second to him, woman. Man is, therefore, universally believed to be more perfect than woman—his achievements prove it. They are without doubt more constant and more firm while women are more changing, more volatile for reasons which I know but won't for the present talk about. Yet for all his greater firmness, a man cannot resist a woman's overtures, her attractions, the lust of the eye which she—sometimes unwittingly—causes. And when that happens, he must follow the instructions of his body and do everything in his power to induce her to pleasure him. Not once, but a thousand times over. So how can you possibly believe that a woman, more variable and susceptible by nature, can resist the onslaughts of a determined seducer? His flatteries, his laments, his gifts, his supplications? Do you really believe that she can hold out against all that? Do you deny that your wife is a woman? A creature of flesh and blood like all the rest? If she is, she must have the cravings, the physical needs that other women have. So why is it that she can withstand them while others can't? You have to admit that it is at least possible, however honest she is, that she may do as others do. And it is quite wrong of you to be so overbearing and categorical in your claims about her."

Ambrogiuolo panted a bit as he finished his speech, and reached out for his wine. He was red and flushed with his own bombast and a hush had fallen over the other three. But Bernabo was not intimidated by Ambrogiuolo's impassioned appeal to his rational side. He knew what he knew and no amount of sophistry or wit or evidence about human nature would sway his belief in what was true beyond doubt. Why, the fact that he was alive because he breathed and his heart beat was no more a fact of his life than Zinevra's fidelity. He was as sure of every claim he made about Zinevra as he was that if he cut his skin, he would find blood.

"I am a merchant, Ambrogiuolo, not a man of elegant words nor a philosopher like you. So I will give you a merchant's answer. I acknowledge that what you say is true of vain and foolish women who have no modesty—but there are judicious women too, who understand that such indiscretion could harm one of the most important relationships in life. And so they can guard their honor better than men, who do not generally stop to consider these issues—largely because they don't really have to—in quite the same way. My wife is of that sort."

"Doubtless," responded Ambrogiuolo savagely, "very few women would indulge themselves in these casual affairs if a horn grew out of their foreheads every time they lapsed. But no horns grow. Not only are there no horns—there's not even the trace or vestige of one to force them to be abstemious. Shame and dishonor lie only in discovery. So women do what they want to do in private and secret and more fool they if they pass up the opportunity. You can be sure that the only chaste woman you'll find is one who hasn't had any offers. Or had her own offers turned down. And I am very sure of myself about this because I've proved it time and again."

He paused a moment and turned even redder than before. The others were still in a haze of mortification, silent. Bernabo wore a lazy, arrogant smile. He had never seen Ambrogiuolo get himself quite so worked up before. He watched Ambrogiuolo pour himself a large glass of wine and pitch it down his throat.

Ambrogiuolo swallowed hard, then he spoke, as if he had never stopped. His face was a deep crimson now, with patches of puce appearing on the cheeks and above his eyebrows, which knit and contorted like crazed worms.

"And I assure you," he thundered, "that if I had access to this saintly wife of yours, I should be as confident of my success with her as with anyone else."

Bernabo felt a flame leap up inside his body—all the way from his toes to his head. He stood up, gripping the edge of the table.

"It would be tedious to protract this discussion anymore. You've had your say, Ambrogiuolo, and I've had mine. We could go on and on ad infinitum, ad nauseam, and it would come to nothing—because you would not change your mind nor I mine. But since you claim to be so accomplished and undefeatable a seducer, I give you my oath that if you can seduce my wife, I will forfeit my head—and if you fail, I'll ask no more from you than one thousand gold florins."

"I don't know what I'll do with your blood, Bernabo, when I win," drawled Ambrogiuolo, thrilled by this unexpected offer, "but if you want me to prove that I'm right, you can pay me five thousand gold florins, which surely must be worth less to you than your head. And though you have not set a time limit, I'll leave immediately for Genoa and guarantee that I'll have strutted with your wife in three months. I will bring back solid, indubitable evidence of my victory. All I ask from you is that you stay away from Genoa and when you write to your wife, say nothing at all about this bet."

"I know my wife," stated Bernabo complacently. "I accept your conditions."

Suddenly—as if a passing fairy had dropped some life-restoring elixir on them—the other three came out of their trance.

"No! No!" they exclaimed in one voice. "A bet like that could have disastrous results. You've both become overheated. Leave it. We've all had too much to eat and drink and we're missing our homes and our wives and . . ."

But neither Bernabo nor Ambrogiuolo would change his mind. They sat down then and there, put the bet into writing, and signed it in the presence of the three uneasy witnesses. And the next day Ambrogiuolo left for Genoa.

Now, in the presence of the sultan and his court, Bernabo shifted uncomfortably in his seat. His head sunk deep into his chest, he shuddered and shivered.

"Within three months Ambrogiuolo had returned. He described my bedchamber in every detail. I refused to take that as proof. He presented me with personal items of Zinevra's clothing. I did not accept them as conclusive evidence. Finally, he described an intimate detail of my wife's body—one which no one but I would know. Then my life turned dark with doubt. I fell into an abyss. I no longer knew anything—if I breathed or if my heart beat or whether, if I cut my skin, I would find blood in it. None of the facts of my life were in place anymore. I gave Ambrogiuolo his money. Five thousand florins. And I did not care about it. I no longer cared about anything, because I no longer knew anything.

"In place of confidence was nothing but doubt. Was I real? Was the life around me a mere illusion? Who was Zinevra? Who was I? We had reflected each other so long, now without a mirror to see myself in and without a reflection to make me real, I knew nothing. Darkness, that was all that was left.

"Do you know how emptiness can fill you and possess you and impel you? I was driven. I returned to Italy to find Zinevra and find out the truth. But as I neared Genoa, I lost my nerve. Blackness swirled around me, emptiness filled me up inside. What twisted, ugly truths would I have to face in the mirror? Her unsightliness made me monstrous, her corruption polluted me. I could not bear the thoughts that jostled the sanity from my brain. My only chance of survival, of recovering my senses, would be to eradicate that distorted and distorting emanation from which I flowed. I decided to have her killed."

As he ended, Bernabo stood up, reeled, and would have fallen, except that several men leaped forward and held him.

The sultan turned to Sicurano, who stood white, lifeless as an alabaster statue. And he saw grief in her face so palpable and so obvious that he averted his gaze, unwilling to peer into the private world of someone who was suddenly a stranger.

"I think," said the sultan, "that we should now hear the story of Ambrogiuolo da Piacenza."

Ambrogiuolo bounced forward, bowing.

"But Your Majesty knows my story already."

"Again!" commanded the emperor, and recalling Sicurano's words, added, "And this time we want no embellishment and all the details. The whole truth, Ambrogiuolo. Just as Bernabo has told us."

Ambrogiuolo glanced at Sicurano, who looked as harsh as the shadow of death. He would not, he could see, have any help from that quarter.

"I have made so much money," thought Ambrogiuolo to himself, "that I can afford to pay back Bernabo's five thousand florins and still have enough to make another quick fortune before returning to Venice. It will be a pinch, losing all that gold—especially at a time when I thought the whole thing was forgotten and behind me. But this is as good a place as any to lose a fortune. And what's five thousand florins compared to my life—which I'll lose without a doubt if the sultan knows I'm lying."

"Well, Your Majesty," he began, "I have seen for the first time today how much damage my account did to this good man Bernabo Lomellin. I admit that everything he says is true. And I will tell my story as honestly as Bernabo has told his."

Ambrogiuolo's Tale

Young Ambrogiuolo da Piacenza of Venice found Bernabo's boasts about his wife beyond belief. Who did Bernabo think he was to take the moral high ground in the matter? He, Ambrogiuolo, was by far the best educated and the highest born of the company, and though he had not joined his companions to belittle his wife, he knew very well that his wife was not averse to the occasional sip of forbidden wine. Even the first woman, mother of humankind, had indulged herself, broken a taboo, succeeded in corrupting her man. It was the first history of man, written in the first book of man. The first woman had been tempted to go against the rules and she had successfully enticed the first man. The world, human history, was balanced on this first truth. Temptation lay at the very foundation of existence—and therefore, so, patently, did woman's susceptibility and her aptitude to corrupt man. Yet Bernabo was calmly denying that his wife had inherited this basic trait from the mother of humankind. Or, for that matter, any weakness at all.

Not only did his claim insult their wives, but worse, it insulted their intelligence. Bernabo was describing someone who could not exist. And he expected them to believe his fantasy.

Well, enough was enough. Ambrogiuolo would teach the arrogant, overbearing creature a lesson for once and for all. Then Bernabo would be forced to concede that he was at the same level as his colleagues and not a cut above.

And so it was that Ambrogiuolo found himself in Genoa, trying to find out what he could about Zinevra. Disconcertingly, everything he heard confirmed Bernabo's boasts. But then, thought Ambrogiuolo, that could be because Bernabo had spread them abroad. But no, her acquaintances confirmed the rumors. Her rejected suitors bewailed her virtue, her rivals, in their resentment, unwillingly recounted her accomplishments, as did her servants in their cups, though servants are known to be the most viciously truthful when talking about their employers—as incisive as a murderer's blade, as ruthless as death in pursuit.

Within a week Ambrogiuolo had to admit to himself that he would have no success with Zinevra. He had to find some way of concealing his defeat. He had said too much, staked too much. And Ambrogiuolo hated losing. Games, boasts, bets, investments—he needed to prove his superiority. To admit to Bernabo that his assertions about human nature had been wrong, and that he had been turned down by Zinevra, would have been unbearable. He would, quite simply, rather have died. Ambrogiuolo admitted freely that he always had to be right, it was his great weakness. But he had been right about one thing in this wretched affair—and that was his ability to captivate women. Before long he had sought out Serafina, a friend and neighbor of Zinevra's, and begun his seduction.

"Does it not annoy you that she is so—superior?" asked Ambrogiuolo, stroking the matron's hair as they lay, sated, in her bed.

"Sometimes, perhaps," giggled Serafina, "but I'm always telling her it's her loss. Look what she's missed this time."

"She must irritate you a little," continued Ambrogiuolo, "with her morality and her achievements and her beauty, surely?"

"Not really," laughed the other. "She doesn't judge others, and her beauty's no threat because she won't look at any man but her husband. So I know she's one person you'll be safe from when I'm away visiting my sister next week."

"Well," growled Ambrogiuolo, "I don't believe that could be true. I'd like to see it for myself."

"And how would you propose to do that?"

"I know!" said Ambrogiuolo, pretending the idea had struck him at that moment. "You could hide me in a large chest and ask Zinevra to look after it while you are away visiting your sister. If no one enters her room for three days, I'll know for sure she's a virtuous woman. If not, then I'll prove I was right and everyone else who knows her was wrong."

"No!" exclaimed Serafina. "That's a terrible thing to do. Zinevra is my friend."

"What if she is? I won't harm her. All I intend to do is see for myself that this woman is the paragon of virtue that everyone claims she is."

"Well," tittered Serafina, "I don't suppose there's much harm in that. And I know that in Zinevra's room you'll be kept safe for me instead of squandering your charms among other women."

"That's true, of course," acknowledged Ambrogiuolo. "Being with Zinevra will keep me amused and imprisoned and I won't be tempted to find comfort in someone else's bed."

"So we'll make it a wager, shall we?" suggested Serafina, her eye to the main chance. "If you win, I'll give you what you want, and if I win, you'll give me what I want."

Ambrogiuolo roared in mock protest and buried his head in Serafina's stomach.

"You know what I want," he thundered into it. "I want you, right here for an entire night and the two days that go with it. And you must not plead exhaustion or turn away from me even once during that time."

"Well, you're a hard taskmaster—and an arrogant one," she said, pouting. "And what will you give me?"

"Anything but myself—because any part of me that's not my own is my wife's, and that is an unalterable fact."

Serafina pouted again. Ambrogiuolo's answer was convenient.

"Well then," she said, "I want a diamond. A large, shiny diamond. Because after a man's undying loyalty, a woman loves a diamond best. And diamonds are more faithful than men."

So the deal was struck and Serafina told Zinevra that she planned to visit her sister in a neighboring district and would be away three days.

"I have a favor to ask you," she pleaded haltingly. "I didn't know, of course, that my husband would not be back when her time came to deliver her baby. Now I'm in a bit of a quandary. He left me with a large wicker chest, you see, and charged me to keep it in my bedroom. I can't take it with me because I don't know what it contains or whether its contents are safe to transport. But if I leave it behind and something goes wrong, I'll be in terrible trouble."

"Do you think it would be safe with me?" offered Zinevra. "In my bedroom? If you do, I'd be happy to look after it for you."

Serafina flushed with pleasure and a large diamond winked and glinted in her mind. "Oh, Zinevra, oh, you're such a friend! I would not have dared to ask . . ."

"Oh, come now," Zinevra laughed, "it's no trouble to let a sealed chest sit in my room! Not even if there's a devil in it, because there's no chance anyone here will open it."

So the chest was carried to Zinevra's room and left under a window. And Ambrogiuolo, who had fixed the roof of the box so that he could open it from the inside and bored it with holes for ventilation, sat inside all day, waiting for night to come.

The first night, when the waiting women had withdrawn from the room and everything was silent, Ambrogiuolo gently unclasped the lock from inside. A candle was burning by the window and he could see by its light that Zinevra was sleeping soundly. Swiftly, he climbed out of the chest and stretched himself, relieved to unfurl his plump little body. Carefully and purposefully he looked around the room, taking in all its details. He walked up to all the pictures, examining them in as much detail as he could, inspected the ground coverings, touching the bedlinen to ascertain its texture. He scrutinized and committed to memory the color, quality, and sound of the objects in the room. Then he went over to the bed and gazed a long time at the sleeping Zinevra—how she lay curved in her bed, her arms embracing a pillow; how she turned, easing her long hair from under her; how she occasionally murmured a prayer as she slept. Then, as dawn began to break, Zinevra tossed and turned and became less peaceful and Ambrogiuolo, the intruder, crept back into the cramped discomfort of his box.

The next night, he tested himself to see what he could remember about the room. Then he looked inside the closets and the boxes and drawers, examined their contents and helped himself to some very private items belonging to Zinevra—a girdle, a ring, a purse, and a gown. For the rest of the night he sat in a comfortable chair and observed Zinevra carefully, perfecting his memory of the habitual nuances and the movements of her sleep—habits so intimate that no one but her husband would know them, not even she herself. Then once again, as dawn broke and the lady became restless, Ambrogiuolo crawled back into his chest and waited.

On the third night, he stalked directly to her bed, lifted the sheet from her, and stared, entranced, at her naked body. Gone was the impersonal scrutiny, the scholarly memorizing, the skillfulness of the hunter stalking his kill. He was mesmerized. He could not move his eyes from the alabaster smoothness of her skin, caressing it up and down with his eyes, longing to crawl into the bed beside her. Then she moved, turning her head onto the pillow and flinging an arm above it. Her beautiful breasts came into view, like small cakes, iced to perfection, topped with little cherries cut in half. And nestling close under the left breast was a mole, fringed with golden hairs so that it glinted like a nugget in the faint light of dawn coming through the window.

"I have it!" he thought, almost shouting the words in his excitement. "I've won the bet."

And he crept back into the box, hardly able to bear the thought of spending a single hour more locked up in the chest.

Serafina was there by midday. She prattled nervously, wondering if her little deception had been found out. When she had confirmed her secret was safe, she could hardly bear to stay another moment, insisting that Zinevra should be relieved immediately of the cumbersome piece of luggage.

"I gave Serafina a diamond as I had promised and we celebrated our success and after that I set off on my way to Paris, where Bernabo was waiting. And the rest you know."

The Sultan's Arbitration

Well, the court was appalled at this hideous tale of treachery. This man Ambrogiuolo had no shame. He had boasted for months about the alleged indiscretions of an innocent woman and continued his lies after she had been killed and fed to wild animals. Nor had he stopped when he learned that Bernabo had lost everything as the result of his deception. By carrying her belongings along, he was ensuring that neither rested in peace, the living dead nor the truly dead.

Seeing their anger, hearing the accusations and criticisms hurled at him by the courtiers, Ambrogiuolo bowed low, to hide his fear and to think fast.

Humility will serve me best now, he decided, and said, "I brought Bernabo to this wonderful place because I was ashamed of what I had done. I thought that here I could make amends without appearing to do him a favor. He is a proud man and would not accept charity. I have lived with my shame and guilt for a long time, but I despise myself even more after hearing Bernabo's account today. I beg you, Bernabo, to accept the five thousand florins of gold that I took from you under false pretenses and to forgive me for what I have done."

He flung himself on the ground in a pose of abject shame.

Bernabo raised his head, his confusion intensified.

"I don't understand, Ambrogiuolo. Are you saying Zinevra is innocent?"

"I am, Bernabo. I am guilty of a terrible deception."

"You are," said Bernabo, rising and pulling himself up to his full stature. "You are the lowest creature ever born. You must be punished and I have no doubt the sultan will find an appropriate way. But as far as I'm concerned, nothing can make up for the death and dishonor of Zinevra."

"Take the money, Bernabo. At least let me pay that back."

"Your money be damned! May you be damned!" screamed the anguished Bernabo, suddenly finding his world restored again but with its vital element missing.

Then the sultan spoke.

"I have rarely seen such evil," he said. "You have destroyed the lives of two good people to feed your own empty pride. And you think money can make up for it."

"I broke no laws, Your Majesty," stammered Ambrogiuolo. "Adultery is not a crime in Italy. And I killed no one. My only misdemeanor was one single lie to defraud Bernabo. And I am now begging him to let me pay him back."

"You have broken every law of humanity!" bellowed the emperor. "And don't you quote the laws of Italy in my court.

The laws of God take precedence in this country and you have broken every one of those. You have told lies—evil lies, lies that caused death and ruin."

The emperor turned to Sicurano, who stood unusually silent and trembling by his side.

"You must guide me, Sicurano," he commanded. "You brought the case to my notice, you are a native of Italy. Tell me what you think."

"Well, sire," Sicurano said, pallid and shivering, "you can see what a lucky woman Zinevra was—with a lover so devoted that he slandered her over four continents for acts she never committed and a husband so trusting that he believed the first falsehood he heard about her after a lifetime knowing she would die rather than betray him. And though both men profess to have loved her, neither has recognized her even though she is standing in front of them. If I have your permission, sire, I will present Zinevra to you now. And I hope Your Lordship will punish the deceiver and pardon the deceived."

The next moment, Sicurano threw herself at the feet of the sultan.

"My Lord, I am Zinevra, slandered by this snake Ambrogiuolo. It was my husband who turned me over to be slaughtered by a servant. And I have wandered six years in fear of my life, as far away from home as I could get, dressed as a man, so that I would not be recognized."

"Your voice," remarked the bemused emperor, "it has changed."

Then Zinevra pulled off her turban and laid it at his feet.

"I am Zinevra," she said, her long, golden hair uncoiling without the turban to contain it. "I am a woman."

She reached for the tie of her cloak and pulled it loose. Her chemise clung to the contours of her body, revealing her woman's form.

"I am a woman," she repeated.

The sultan watched the transformation in amazement. He had never once doubted that Sicurano was who he appeared to be: a man—a very talented man.

He waited a moment, expecting the wisps of confusion to disperse and clarity to come. This was perhaps a dream from the early hours of morning. Any moment now, he would wake up and find that he had experienced a strange and detailed dream—a vision, almost—and he would investigate the whole business of Ambrogiuolo and Bernabo. But when a few moments later the scene did not change or vanish and he found himself still on his throne and not in his bed, he knew he was firmly in reality though it really had so much of the fantastical and wondrous in it. And as he forced his mind to ingest and process the transformation of a man—and a pretty constant companion of his at that—into a woman, he realized quite what a magnificent man Sicurano really was. And that this exceptional man had really been a woman meant that the woman was truly twice the paragon of virtue that anyone had ever claimed she was, for to be a woman and yet be twice as good as a man . . . oh, stop!

It was enough that he knew the facts now, startling as they were, and he spoke in high praise of this man . . . er, woman . . . who had been his companion and adviser and lieutenant for five years; the model of manners and good breeding, of skill and efficiency, of modesty and virtue. There was no praise high enough for her. And he could think of no man who deserved her. But he knew that she loved Bernabo and like most women was susceptible to the vulnerability of others and had a tendency to forgive.

"Leave the court," he commanded, his eyes twinkling, "and from now on come here dressed only as a woman. A proper train of women should attend Lady Zinevra, and when she returns I will hand her over to her husband, whom she has forgiven."

Zinevra bowed, thanked the sultan, and saluted him for the last time as his lord governor and friend, Sicurano da Finale.

Bernabo flung himself down in front of her, begging her to forgive him. He could see how wrong he had been but was boundlessly grateful to God that she was alive. Even if she refused to forgive him or to take him back, he would spend the rest of his days thanking Him for her safety. But Zinevra lifted Bernabo up and embraced him compassionately.

"You are my husband," she said simply, "and now that I know the facts, I will try to understand why you doubted my loyalty."

"The wretch Ambrogiuolo should be tied to a stake," commanded the emperor, "his bare flesh anointed with honey, and exposed to the sun on the hills in the city, there to remain until his flesh falls off his bones."

All those present nodded their agreement as the sultan continued: "And his entire estate both here and in Italy which should amount to no less than ten thousand doubloons should go to the Lady Zinevra. As a token of my own esteem, I will give her gifts of gold, silver, and precious jewels worth at least twice that amount in loving memory of my faithful friend Sicurano da Finale."

. .

That night the sultan arranged the most magnificent feast for the reunion of Zinevra and Bernabo Lomellin.

"This," he sighed sentimentally, "is the first time I have held a marriage ceremony and a birth ceremony all in one. For though my dear friend Sicurano has left us, he has left us with the product of his own body—Lady Zinevra."

As a final gift, the sultan gave Zinevra a ship so that she could return with her husband to Genoa.

And what became of Ambrogiuolo? Ah, well, the guests at the feast said that the honey on his body attracted wasps and horseflies and other vicious insects in so many of their thousands that they sucked the blood from his flesh and the flesh from his bones that same day and his remains were left hanging on the stake as a sign of his vileness.

Rubies for a Dog

Once there was an emperor, much loved and much respected. But when he put his faithful old adviser the grand wazir into prison, and worst of all, told nobody the reason why, people wondered about his sense of fair play. Still, everyone accepted that emperors can be erratic at times and that the wazir had probably said something so offensive that it did not bear repetition. So everyone in the kingdom looked the other way. Everyone, that is, except the wazir's daughter, Samira. She refused to sit idle in the halls of her father's sumptuous mansion while he, the provider of all this luxury, languished in a dank cell with chains locking both his limbs and his lips. But try as she might, she could not get her father to tell her anything, and without the facts she could do nothing.

"You are my only child," the wazir said sadly, "and I thank God for you. I will not risk your life and limb by telling you. If I had a son he would do what is necessary to clear my name. But I cannot send a daughter."

When Samira's father refused her help because she was a woman, she felt humiliated and useless. She crept back to her castle and wept, and cursed the narrow vision of men who bound women to their homes then considered them incapable of achieving anything outside.

"If I visit my father," she thought miserably, "I will only remind him that he has no son while I, his wretched daughter, incapable of helping him, remain ensconced in his mansion, swathed in silk, decking myself in gold and jewels and always in danger of jeopardizing his reputation. As far as he's concerned, the only good I can do is to live a blame-free life so that people call him a man of noble birth and virtuous character."

A few days later, Samira received a message from her father. Was all well with her? He was grateful for the food she had sent and he did not wish to impose a visit on her. But he needed to know she was safe and well. A message would be enough.

Samira longed to see her father—but how could she? Her woman's body, her long hair, her feminine attire, would be anathema to him. To see in her what could have been but was definitely not must be unbearable to him. She stood staring at herself in the mirror—exquisite as a peri, tall and straight as a cypress tree, rosy-cheeked—from head to toe the essence of beauty. Yet she hated every part of herself. In a rage, she picked up a small dagger and began to rip away at her clothes. Then she looked with pleasure at the velvets and chiffons and beaded silks lying in fragments on the floor. But when she looked up, her reflection still mocked her.

"*I'm still here,*" it taunted. "*Still beautiful and still female. Now what will you do to deny me?*"

Samira put the sharp blade to her head and long silken strands of hair slithered, lifeless, to the ground. For a moment she fancied she saw a woman reflected in the soft sheen of her tresses—her mother. "*You are right,*" she seemed to say, "*I approve of your plan.*"

Reassured, Samira ran to her father's bedchamber and began looking in his wardrobe. Amid the brocades and the velvets she searched and foraged until at last she found a small bundle of starched pink muslin, sparkling with silver formica from the sea. She undid the knot that tied it, and there it was! The outfit her father wore when he went wandering amid the crowds of Constantinople to learn what the people of his great emperor Azad Bakht were thinking. It was useful for a wazir to know whether people were content or discontent, what pleased them about their sovereign and what made them unhappy, whether they thought him wise or whether they declaimed a folly or two that had crept into his character. Then the wazir would act on it. Cleverly and diplomatically, he would reshape the criticisms and filter the contents of his findings into the emperor's ear to mold him into an even better ruler, just as he had done for his father before him. No fool was our worthy wazir—until this last time. What had gone wrong that time? For he had made a mistake that he would probably never have the chance to rectify. That is, if Azad Bakht and the wazir had their way. But Samira had her own ideas on the matter.

Carefully she dressed herself in the flowing overcoat and baggy trousers her father wore to go out among the people. They were of plainer cloth and not so highly embroidered; a little duller, because the thread of the embroidery was dyed in the colors of flowers and vegetables rather than gold and silver; clothes that would not set her apart from the average merchant or businessman.

"Apart from the turban," she thought, "it's all much the same. I fit these clothes as well as I fit my own. But the turban feels cumbersome on my head just as Father's duties must weigh him down."

Then Samira made her way to the dungeon.

"Your daughter has sent me," she said, deepening her voice. "I am her sworn brother and therefore your son. I am to be your champion and free you from this odious place. I beg you, tell me why Emperor Azad Bakht imprisoned you and how you can make amends."

The wazir looked perplexed. He could not tell a stranger, even if that stranger was sworn to be his champion. What if he were the emperor's agent provocateur and not Samira's ambassador at all? He shook his head sadly. Samira had chosen well and he felt a fatherly warmth for this boy although he barely knew him.

"There is something about you that I feel I can trust, but I can't betray my emperor," he said firmly. "He has commanded me to say nothing."

"Father!" cried Samira, removing her turban. "Don't you recognize me? I am your daughter! Please let me help you."

The old wazir's eyes filled with tears. Tears of sadness, tears of love, tears of pride. And for a while he could not bring himself to speak.

"My child," he said eventually, clutching her to him, "you have cut your beautiful hair, the legacy of your mother, and you've given it up for me. It must have broken your heart."

Samira nodded. "Yes, but I would rather serve the living than the dead," she replied. "I have lost my mother, I am desperate to keep my father. So please, Father, tell me why you are here."

The wazir sighed. He was bursting with pride at his daughter's bravery and quite overcome by her devotion and determination.

"Then listen," he began. "One day some merchants from Badakhshan visited our court with gifts for the emperor. Among them was a wonderful ruby. It seemed to hold the depth of an ocean, an ocean at sunset, when it is red and luminous because it has sucked the fire from the sun itself. And every time Azad Bakht looked at it, he forgot everything else. There is no doubt this was a rare gem. It captivated everyone who looked at it.

"You know how it is with emperors—they often lose the distinction between the important and the less important. They are easily diverted by games and women and trinkets. Then it is up to their servants to remind them of the important things. And we tried, many of us, to point out to Azad Bakht that the ruby was excessively distracting—but would he listen? He began to suspect that we had our eye on the ruby, that we wanted it for ourselves. Even that we were jealous of this inanimate stone. It was almost as if—God forgive me and cast dust in my mouth, but it must be said—it was almost as if Azad Bakht had begun to worship this stone. He could not bear to be without it. He would abandon meetings with important emissaries in order to have a quick peep at the stone. He would hold up vital proceedings to show off the gem to state visitors. Inevitably, one day matters went too far.

"A neighboring king was visiting to ask for Azad Bakht's support in a war against another king. The battle was a personal one and Azad Bakht would never have agreed in the normal course of affairs because this third king has always been faithful to us. But the visiting king saw his chance and seized it when Azad Bakht flaunted the ruby to him and in tones at once awed and arrogant demanded, "Tell me, have you such a jewel in your possession?" Well, from then on they talked of nothing but the great gems of the world and how this ruby must be among the greatest ones. Before the meeting had ended, the clever visitor had procured Azad Bakht's help to fight his personal battle—our forces for his battle against a king who had never done us harm. Well, it was too much to stand by and accept. The king left, knowing he had outmaneuvred our young emperor. It could be terrible for his reputation.

"That night when I went into the streets, the story had already gotten around. The people are forgiving, Samira, but not when their lives and their beloved country are at stake. They talked that night, talk to shame the bones of an old servant like me. Azad Bakht may be young, they said, but we've had boy emperors before now who have brought great glory to the land. Little do they know, a boy emperor is more likely to achieve glory than a young man, for his ego is not yet full blown and his ears more open to the wisdom of older men.

"I knew that night that I must tell the emperor as bluntly as possible how the ruby was affecting him, that he must put his passion in perspective or he would do himself and his empire dreadful harm. That night, alone with Azad Bakht in his bed-chamber and after all the courtiers had left, I had my chance to speak.

"I admit I was nervous, but the wazir is the servant of the emperor and the emperor of the state and the state of the people and the people of God. So you see, I was at the bottom of a long list. Soft words and gentle advice had no effect on Azad Bakht and, I don't know—I suppose it was partly the anger of hearing my emperor criticized, partly the humiliation of withdrawing our word to the visiting king, partly my own earlier failure—but my blood was on the boil and nothing drives a man to greater risk than simmering rage. Well, whatever it was that night, it drove me to an action that has reduced me to this.

"I stood by the elbow of Azad Bakht and I said in as firm a voice as I could muster, 'Your Majesty, Shadow of the Eternal, Refuge of the World, Recipient of the Wisdom of the Almighty, I have something important to tell you but it will fall heavy on your gracious ear.' "

" 'What is it?' said Azad Bakht, growing a little crabby, for it was late at night. He rubbed the great ruby against his cheek, then reached out and placed it in a niche directly above his bed. I noticed that the exquisitely inscribed calligraphy of a verse from the Koran had been removed to make room for the wretched stone. It saddened me.

" 'I will tell you,' I said, 'if you promise to spare my life.'

" 'Yes, yes,' replied Azad Bakht, getting impatient. 'Your life is safe. Now, get on with it.'

"Well, you can imagine how I felt. Clearly the emperor was in no mood to hear criticism—and then not as harshly as I meant to put it—but I had no option because I had decided carefully on my words and methods.

" 'Well, Your Majesty,' I said, looking boldly into the emperor's eyes, 'it is about the ruby.'

"Quite unconsciously, Azad Bakht reached out and clutched the stone, holding it defensively to his heart.

" 'Oh, you're not still complaining about my fabulous ruby, are you?'

" 'It does not become a great emperor like you to give such importance to a mere stone,' I continued.

" 'A mere stone?' shouted the emperor, holding up the ruby for me to see. 'Look how it sparkles and casts its light. It is sublime, it is supernatural. How can anyone but an idiot describe it as a "mere stone"? The like of it was never encountered anywhere else.'

" 'Not so, my liege.' I quaked to hear my voice clipped and curt, but say it I must, 'For I have heard tales that a merchant of Nishapur has a dog whose collar is studded with twelve rubies each one as large and as perfect as this one.'

"Azad Bakht gasped and clutched his throat. Horrified, I rushed up to help him. I thought he was going to choke. It was as if my words had knocked the breath from him. But he pushed me away. He gasped, spluttered, and turned the color of the luscious quinces of Lebanon. Then quite suddenly he regained control.

" 'You have insulted me and that makes you a traitor,' he said in a voice that was quiet and very deadly. I have never seen my emperor so cold and so terrifying as he was at that moment. 'Traitors die a hideous death, but you have served my family faithfully and wisely for many years and I have given you my word. Therefore, you will live out the rest of your life in the dungeons of the old fort.'

" 'My liege,' I whispered, throwing myself to my knees, 'your wish is my command. But will my daughter be safe?'

" 'Your daughter is my sister,' the emperor told me. His words were spoken like a true monarch. 'She will be under my protection and may, if she chooses, move into the royal palace for her own security. If she prefers, however, she may stay in your mansion and I will pronounce her a ward of the emperor.'

"Thankfully, I rose and opened the doors. At my own command, the royal guard escorted me to the prison where I am today. And if it were not for the graciousness of my emperor, my punishment could have been horrendous. I could have had my eyes gouged out with hot pokers, been subjected to several hundred strokes of the lash, had my tongue amputated . . ."

Samira shuddered and put her hands to her father's lips.

"Please, Father," she begged, "we need not dwell on such horrors now."

The wazir shook his head. "It is important for us both to acknowledge how lucky I am. The emperor has been merciful. My body is whole, though I am growing weak, and a life in this cell is no great hardship when you send me wonderful food each day and all the parts of my body are intact. I haven't many years of life left—those I can eke out in relative peace, praying and repenting and nourishing my soul."

Samira stood up and stalked back and forth for a while, building up the courage to put her question to her father. She could feel his eyes watching her, alert for her request. No, her father had not lost any of his faculties, physical or mental.

"Father," she said at last, "I want your blessings."

"You have those always," cut in the wily wazir before she could proceed with her request.

Samira began to lose her nerve. Then she recovered herself and with greater determination than before, began again.

"I want to go to Nishapur to find the dog with the ruby collar. I want your permission and your blessings."

"Do you know what you're asking?" demanded the wazir. "The city of Nishapur is far, far away, in Khorasan. You have to cross tracts of desert and face fighting hordes who know as little of mercy as they do of palaces. Only an army has any chance of getting past them."

"Two strangers stand more chance than an army," retorted Samira. "An army would put them on their guard. A caravan would alert them to infinitely greater treasures than one body can carry. But a single young man with an old attendant will pose no threat to warrior tribes. Besides, we know from the stories of the great minstrels that wit wins many a battle before it is ever fought."

"Ah, Samira, Samira," lamented the wazir, "the lack of a mother has done you more harm than I ever imagined. You read books on battle and look deep into the *Mirror of Princes* and you talk back to your father. Well, I brought you up so I must take the blame. Perhaps it would have been wiser to hand you over to my sister, then perhaps I would not be in this dilemma today."

"Father, you have given me everything I ever needed. You have nurtured in me the creativity and determination of a woman and a heart as brave as a she-lion's. In archery and swordsmanship I was the best among my companions. But people think a woman's body is frail and vulnerable—I concede that. That is why I have to dress like this. Isn't it ironic that I have to dress as a man in order to discover the full potential of my womanhood?''

The wazir looked at his daughter with new eyes. He could not deny this young woman, this brave and wise young woman, the chance of self-discovery. He sighed so deeply, his frail frame shuddered with the force of it. He would probably never see the girl again. Flesh of his flesh, fruit of his loins, beloved gift of his dead wife.

"But," he thought, "the greatest gift a parent can give a child is the approval to do what she must. Yet how difficult it is to give. 'Yes, and I bless your efforts'—how hard it is to say those words. But I must say them because it is quite obvious Samira has thought a lot about the matter and I have no wish to stop my daughter fulfilling herself."

The wazir raised his hand and put it on Samira's head.

"Go with my blessings," he said. "And never forget who you are and why you go."

Samira threw her arms around her father. Tears filled her eyes and, promising him she would remember all the advice he had given her over the years, she left the dungeon.

Up in her castle she made ready for the journey. She would need a few spare sets of clothes. A trusted servant was sent out to acquire these. She would need provisions, merchandise for trade, gifts to pacify the nomad robbers and other brigands. And gold coins and gems which she had sewn into the stiffened hems of her coat and other robes. Finally, accompanied by the faithful servant, she set off on her journey.

The road was long and arduous and there were nights when they slept between the vast skies and the shifting desert sands, as huge, radiant stars hung in clustering branches above them, bright as the torches that lit the richest mansions of Constantinople. Occasionally they would hear the tinkle of a hospitable camel bell and a kindly tribesman would raise them from their sandy bed and take them to his home. Then there were the easier nights in plush and humble caravanserais, travelers' houses built along the trunk roads.

"God be praised," Samira and her servant often said to each other. "The Prophet advised his followers well when he commanded them to provide resting places for travelers. Clearly he had experienced the travails of the desert when he issued the code of hospitality to the tribesmen."

Finally they arrived in Khorasan, traveling on, frequently asking for direction, until they reached the city of Nishapur, where they took rooms in a modest but comfortable inn. At breakfast on the very first day, Samira spoke to the landlord.

"Is there a particular quarter in this town where the jewelers have their shops?"

"There might be and there might not be," replied the dour fellow. "What is it you seek? To sell or to buy?"

"To look, at first," responded Samira jauntily, "and then, if I find your Nishapuri goods worthwhile, perhaps to trade. A little buying, a little selling. That's where the fun of business lies."

"Oh, the arrogance of the young," grumbled the innkeeper. "Don't be so proud of your wealth and your youth, for the colors of such garments fade soon enough. As to your cheeky remarks—you'll not find better jewelers anywhere than in our Nishapur bazaars."

"What!" exclaimed Samira, enjoying the man's irritation. "Are you claiming that your jewelers have better gems than the ones from Badakhshan, finer gold than the Arabian isles, diamonds more exquisite than the ones from India?"

"I do," insisted the innkeeper. "Our jewelers cast their nets far and wide and haul in the treasures of the deepest, most obscure places. You have only to see their caravans when they return, twenty guards at front and back, horses and camels creaking with the weight of it all."

"I've seen many caravans in my day," laughed Samira, "and I have no wish to see any more. But I will take a stroll around your market to see if your boasts are true."

And so saying, she set off in search of the merchant with the dog. She walked the streets of the city all day, asking questions openly, making inquiries but finding out nothing until on the fourth day she came across a large store displaying such fabulous jewels that she was quite overwhelmed by their beauty. There were fat emeralds, winking, blinking pools of green; rubies like luminous roses and hibiscus; diamonds so large they were like mounds of white light; sapphires bluer than the sky after a rainstorm; topazes like sunbursts; aquamarines as clear as the turquoise seas; lapis lazuli, veined and speckled in gold; amethysts, jet, turquoise, amber . . .

"The Emperor Azad Bakht would go mad here," she thought wickedly. "He would transport the entire store and its contents to Constantinople."

She shut her eyes and placed her fingers on the lids to shut out the harsh glare of the stones. When she opened them again, they focused on a low bed on which slept a large hound. An attendant smoothed its beautiful red tresses, while another fanned it, waving away the flies. A third stood a little way behind the others, watchful that the dog's dishes of food and drink were fresh and full. And around the neck of this elegant, pampered hound of Afghanistan was a large collar of velvet studded with twelve enormous rubies.

She had found him! Her father's savior! Now she could prove to Azad Bakht that her father's words were the truth and not an idle insult. But first she must ask the dog's owner why he had made a collar of rubies for a dog.

Without delay, Samira introduced herself as a visiting merchant to the owner of the shop, an elegant and gracious young man who invited her to eat and drink with him.

"But I am curious," said Samira when the pleasantries were over, "to find out more about your dog. Why does he wear a collar of rubies?"

"The dog is called Wafadar—Loyal One," began the merchant of Nishapur. "The best friend man can ever have."

Then the merchant told Samira that during his travels as a boy he had encountered seven misfortunes. Each time Wafadar had saved his life, or befriended him.

"When I lay ill and hungry by the wayside, the dog guarded me from man and beast; when I was set upon by brigands and my companions abandoned me, he fought by my side. When, twice, I lost my fortunes and suddenly had no friends in the world, Wafadar stayed by me, finding food for himself and for me by hunting fowl and wild deer. When finally at the age of twenty-six I made a fortune so vast that ten lifetimes could not make a dent in it, nothing was so precious to me as Wafadar.

"My old friend's traveling days were over. He was tired and deserved to rest. I decided to settle down for once and all and resolved to give my faithful old companion every luxury in my power, so ostentatiously that people would come to see the dog and ask me to tell his story. Then I would have the chance to extol his virtues and pay him homage."

Samira was moved to tears by the story of the merchant.

"His story has spread far and wide," she said when she had managed to collect herself. "It is because of him that my father, the Wazir of Constantinople, is languishing in the dungeons of Emperor Azad Bakht."

And Samira told the merchant who she was and why she had come in search of him, dressed in men's clothes.

"I am sorry that your father suffered as a result of telling Wafadar's story," said the merchant quietly, "and I would like to help in any way I can."

The dog was awake now and lifted his head, then rose to his noble feet and ambled over to his master.

Immediately the merchant took a fine piece of meat from his jeweled plate and fed it to Wafadar. The dog picked up the offering and looked at his owner with love in his eyes and Samira saw the love reflected in the eyes of the merchant. Quietly, she looked on as the merchant stroked and fondled his dog and the dog rested his long, graceful muzzle on the merchant's knee.

"I would like to help you," said the merchant, "because I admire your efforts. You combine wisdom and courage with a soft heart and single-minded dedication. I didn't know women like you existed."

"Perhaps," murmured Samira, "because women are not often given the chance to prove their potential."

But the merchant was too preoccupied with his next thought to hear her.

"Come and stay with me in my humble home," he said, "and let us discuss your next step." He looked at Wafadar. "And you, old friend, would you be willing to go on another journey for your master's sake?"

Wafadar licked his master's hand and stood up, suddenly playful.

"He agrees," smiled the merchant. "He agrees to accompany Samira to Constantinople to plead her father's case. You have lived up to your name, Samira—a true friend and companion. In my country, poets write of a little white dove called Samira, who proved her friendship by traveling far and wide to repay a human who once saved her life. It strikes me that you have done the same."

That night, in the halls of the merchant's manor, Samira fell in love, and when the merchant proposed marriage, she accepted.

"But only on condition that you agree to come and live in Constantinople," she insisted.

The merchant agreed and the next day they embarked on the return journey, which this time was far more comfortable than Samira had imagined possible.

On her return home, Samira's first visit was to her father.

"I am back, Father, and I have with me the dog with the collar of twelve rubies and the man who owns him. What will the emperor say to that?"

The old wazir fell on his daughter's neck and wept with gratitude for her safe return.

"My days were hell and my nights hellfire while you were away," he confessed. "I imagined that you had been attacked by every evil and besieged by every conceivable misfortune. I felt sure I would never see you again. I would have thanked God a million times every moment of the day for the rest of my life, even if you had returned alone and without the means to free me."

"Shame, Father," laughed Samira. "You have very little faith in your daughter."

Then Samira sought an audience with the emperor and requested permission to bring a companion. The audience was granted and Samira and the merchant told Azad Bakht the whole story. He described how Samira had left home dressed as a man to redeem her father's honor. She had traveled all the way from Constantinople to Nishapur, across dangerous territory, braving nature, man, and beast until at last she had found the merchant and his dog. Then the merchant told his own tale of the dog's loyalty.

"And now, Your Majesty, we are here to present you with the facts and beg a reprieve for Samira's father, the grand wazir."

"I have never heard such an incredible story!" exclaimed Azad Bakht. "And I thank God that my wazir was not harmed or put to death!"

Immediately he ordered the release of the wazir, and in the presence of his family and his most important courtiers he begged his forgiveness.

"And all this," concluded the emperor, "has been achieved because of the efforts of a devoted daughter."

"A daughter," thought Samira alone in her chamber that night, smoothing her soft fabrics to her skin, inhaling the perfumed atmosphere of her room, sliding against the silk of her bedclothes, "who is very happy to be a woman now that she has shown what womankind can achieve."

The Legend
of Mary Ambree

That was the last night Mary Ambree would ever think of roses and wine when the sun's blood smeared the sky. From that night on, she knew that the breast of the heavens had been gashed open and those who saw and took heed died a sort of death and had to be reborn. And when she looked down at the brave sergeant-major, her beloved, she saw clearly that same heavenly gash on his breast. My God! It was reflected in the skies themselves. Then Mary knew the time had come.

"I wonder," she mused, distracted, "would it have been different if I had known I would fulfill my yearning over the dead body of my sweetheart?"

And her mind ran again along those childhood days, recalling the sweet triumph of knowing, as she watched the boys play, that her limbs were stronger than theirs though her movements remained more lissome, that her arms could carry the same weight and her back the same burden—if not an even greater one. How she hated that skirt winding itself around her muscular legs, her sturdy ankles, like a great, snaking rope. A rope called "womanhood" with which her parents were pledged to bind her.

"Now, now, Mary, not that, lass, 'tis for the boys, that game, not for a young woman." "Tch, tch, Mary lass, where's your sense? You'll never find you a husband if you don't stop that."

But why should she stop when she could wield a weapon and hit a target with the best of them? She had worn the soldiers down with her demands from the time she was just ten, until they had taught her their skills—sometimes for the price of a kiss. Then her breasts grew and the blood came and with it more admonitions and curses and women's company. She was forced to watch how her mother, along with her contemporaries, manipulated the men and maneuvred the money; how she rallied the rations and piled up the provisions. Occasionally, she even pinched the odd penny to save, from an already stretched budget, adding more to it, besides, by pleading ignorance and stupidity before her husband.

Furthermore, she saw the same skills budding in the younger women as they turned their sweethearts into husbands. How the sturdiest of them went limp-wristed to bring out the chivalry in her man! How the laziest could somehow convey her commitment to industry! How each one preached and demanded openness and honesty from her husband and children when she never had the slightest intention of practicing either herself. And good luck to them one and all—because, Mary knew, without their little deceptions and flatteries, where would they be? The lot of women was not one any man could have worked so well with. Women were invested with sturdier souls—all the more frustrating for having to match them to weak bodies and inferior minds.

Mary hated being reminded of the frailties of women, their weaknesses, their susceptibility to evil. And by the very men who were manipulated by them each day. Besides, if the accusations were true, then Mary was a man in a woman's body, for she did not care a bit for the running of houses or the putting by of money with which to buy lace. She wanted to see the world! She wanted glory! She wanted to be honored. England had a queen—so for that matter had Scotland. That was enough proof to her that notwithstanding her body, she could achieve her desires.

"Men act, women talk," her father said, and most men agreed as they slumped down after a hard day's work to snore. "No wonder their work stretches from sunrise to sundown and even further."

Nor did Mary ever hear them—her mother and her contemporaries—correct the fallacy. The sham suited them. Craftiness in a woman was not attractive, it had to be disguised. A simple, hardworking woman fared far better. That was the way to be. Oh, the wiles and guiles and dark little ways of women! Mary watched them but they were not for her! Not for her the brews of the widow in the woods, or the protective talismans of the fairy man in the wilds. God's guidance and an upright life would see Mary through. She would not resort to sham and petty trickery. The truth was, women did little to improve their own lot in a proper way. They were content with scoring small

points, with red ribbons and frippery and the well-timed expo-
sure of the blossoming flesh above an ankle or an ample bosom.
But not Mary: she sought glory, victory, the greater good.

She would bind her small breasts with the rags used for
household chores, clench her skirts between her legs, then posture, shoulders squared, bust thrust out like a pigeon-chested
soldier. Oh, how she coveted the debonair uniforms of the
soldiers—and their cavalier headdress.

The sergeant-major used to let her wear his.

He was a man in a million, the sergeant-major. He would
hand over his spare uniform to her as much to show her he had
a spare, mind you—which was a rare thing. He had bought it
from a cast-off old soldier who had barely a limb left to wear it
on. And he let her dress in it—even helped her, caressing her
body some of the while and for the rest watching, watching her
every move, every action, as he watched in battle for the very
shadow of the enemy stirring the bushes on the other side.
Then he would stand in front of her—a reflection, for their
bodies were so alike—and they would embrace and kiss. There
would generally be a brief scuffle and sometimes the sergeant-
major won and sometimes Mary and they would fall all in a
heap. Once down, they would strip each other like the men
who become vultures after a battle, stripping their fellow man
bare of the treasures that are real and those that are precious
only because love makes them so. That was the part of war
Mary found repulsive.

"But no," said the sergeant-major. "There is another soul.
A surviving, predatory soul that comes out when you have to
kill your fellow man. And you look at him and see in his place
an unchristian devil—a horned monster who will kill you if you
don't kill him first."

His eyes blazed, his cheeks flushed, and Mary could see he was in the possession of that other kind of creature. Then suddenly, he slumped. "It takes time for such a desperate soul, so bent upon survival, to loosen its grip. And just as well, for if it went too fast, so many of us would lose the spirit to forage among the dead, demons or friends, to find what we can to sustain us while we're still out there fighting. For the dead don't need it anymore, but the living do." Then his face would become soft and mellow and his eyes fill with tears. "And oh, Mary Ambree, how willingly and sweetly the dead do give."

"And is every soldier more skilled than I?" demanded Mary.

The sergeant-major guffawed—a raw, deep laugh that was wrenched from his deepest core. "If only! If only, Mary Ambree! No, indeed, for men sell their lads so young, they have less hair on their cheeks than you. A boy's life for less money than would see the rest of the family through the winter."

Gently, he stroked her downy cheeks against the growth. His tongue often flicked the fluff by the sides of her lips. Her sturdy, boyish body he loved profoundly, but the fine, soft hair on the upper lip he found a special treat. And Mary, who had never cared a jot for smoothness of skin and limb or fullness of breast and hip like the girls around her, lay back and enjoyed his enjoyment, her body growing heavy and languorous and open to his ministrations.

So it was that only too soon, when the sergeant-major had to dress himself up again and follow his fortune into the next battle, Mary convinced him that she should go too. She would look after him, she would fight by his side, she would mop his brow when no one cared for any but themselves. And the army would get two for the price of one. So Mary Ambree accompanied her sweetheart when he joined Alexander Farnese, the Prince of Parma, in his fight against the Dutch. To look at, she wasn't a soldier, just the sergeant-major's woman, but she got to see the world of men and the excitement, adventure, and challenge she had yearned for. At the end of each day they exulted to find each other alive and crept away to a silent place to talk of the dangers each had survived.

Now he lay dead and a part of her dead with him. But perhaps she needed that part to die before the other could be born.

Slowly Mary shed her blouse, her bodice, her skirt, and stood stark naked under the sky, alone except for the dead.

"Now, my love," she said, "I stand before you with nothing to hide and nothing more to give save devotion."

She stood there for a while, clinging to her nakedness, nothing but grief and death pervading her being. Nothing was left. Nothing.

Then slowly, out of nothingness, resolve began to form. It moved her limbs, it informed her actions, and she knew what she would do. Without hesitation she undressed her lover, gazing on his beloved naked body a last time. And his words came back to her: "Oh, Mary Ambree, how willingly and sweetly the dead do give."

She felt the tears scorch rivulets down her face, through thick battle grime and muck as she dressed herself for her new role.

She clothed herself in buff—the fabric that most announced bravery, and over it a shirt of mail. She crowned her head with a helmet of proof and girded her side with a strong-armed sword. Over her right hand she drew a gauntlet. Then, armed with sword and target, she stood by his body, the sword held high and pointing skyward.

Mary Ambree had died and was remade.

"Listen to me, men!" she called.

The men saw that the voice came from the clothes of the sergeant-major. But though it sounded straight from Mary's breast, loud and deep and clear, they knew it was not the resounding bass of their leader. Those who had seen him fall thought it was his ghost, the figure looked so like him. Yet they rallied. It was as if the clothes made the man. Her hand ran unconsciously from breasts to genitals as if expecting the one to have gone, the other to have grown.

"I am Mary Ambree," said the lass. "Many of you know me, for I have fought by the side of my sweetheart who lies dead here, killed by the enemy. I've traveled with you and I've foraged for food and fed many of you, for that falls to a woman to do—even when her face is covered in gunpowder smoke, like yours, and she has fought like you to save her life and that of others. For the battlefield, you know, is not much different from the home. A woman's work counts for nothing, it seems, if she does not add to all her other labors the chores of lighting a fire, toiling with a ladle and putting food on plates for hungry mouths. Men, children, what's the difference when it comes to filling their faces and their bellies? But by the blood on this sword, I swear I'll avenge my sweetheart's blood and finish his work."

The cheer that went up must have reached the skies.

"Am I to take it that you will follow me, then?"

There was another roar of assent. Three thousand men had seen her fight at the very forefront of the battle. Three thousand men decided to follow her faithfully where she led them, though a few of them were carried on the determination and enthusiasm of the others. And in return Mary Ambree made them a promise.

"Before you perish or come to any danger from the enemy, this hand and this life of mine shall set you free."

Mary's cooking days were over. She never touched a spoon or a scrap of food from then on, except to eat.

Well, the trumpets sounded and the drums beat but the loudest of all was the roar of the cannon as it boomed Mary's intent. And she held to her promise. For every one man of hers that the enemy killed, Mary killed a score of them. Oh, her body was more strong and her heart more brutal than the best of them! Her band would look at her in battle and draw strength from her, for never had they seen a fighter so fierce, so determined, so passionate as Mary. Where, they wondered, was the woman's heart that beat within her? Because they did not know that the heart that beat within Mary was a warrior's heart and it knew no gender—only the resolve of victory, spurred on by the sweetness of revenge.

Sometimes they would see the tears flow, copiously and quickly down her perpetually smoke-smeared face, her brow furrowed as she pushed back the strands of hair straggling about her face and pulled a bloody, grimy cuff across her nose and eyes to wipe away the snot, obscure the tears. But they were never sure—were those tears from the poison fumes of smoke and smut, or from personal grief? They knew for sure only that she was crying, when she knelt over one of her own men dying or dead and said she was sorry she had not fulfilled her pledge to save them from death as she had promised. But then, in a flash of fury, fortified and more furious than ever, she would spring to her feet and take on the other side with a savagery that was terrifying even to her own men. Perhaps that was what kept even the most disgruntled man loyal.

At times like that Mary seemed to grow—larger and larger, taller and taller, her sword so long and bright there was an aura around her that dazzled because it had been sent, doubtless by divinity, and the enemy could not penetrate it. There were stories of ancient women warriors so powerful and incisive that men called them goddesses—Morrigu, Minerva, Maebh—then there was their own Mary.

The battle continued for many days. Food became scarce. Limbs grew weary. Bodies fell all around, burst with bullets, slashed with swords. The minds of men grow unhappy in these circumstances, for they see their own faces on those wounded dead. And though Mary grew more wiry and fiery and big, her hunger became twofold, for it came from both her heart and her belly. She seemed to be here and there and everywhere all at once, while her men grew slower and heavier. Then one of them decided that mercenary as he was, he was doing no wrong to sell himself to the enemy side. But in order for them to believe that he was genuine, and that it was not a trick of the clever and courageous captain of England to infiltrate their ranks, he had to give them clear proof. The man racked his brains for hours, until it struck him—the obvious. It had been staring him in the face, jolting his body, blasting his brain all the time he was here. He was the gunner. He had charge of the munitions. He would give away the powder and the bullets that aided Mary Ambree in her fight. He would hand them over to the enemy. Then, when they saw how poorly the English fought the next morning, he would creep over and join them. Oh! He'd be a hero! He surely would. And the Dutch would trust him and welcome him, for who would be stupid enough to give away the last piddling bits of ammunition left to their side if they meant to continue there? And though these past few days had been the worst the Dutch had seen, they knew that Mary was coming to the end of her provisions and ammunition.

When Mary went to bed that night her heart was dizzy—flying one moment with the excitement of taking the Castle Gaunt, leaden the next with the knowledge that it would mean certain death for many of her band. The three thousand had dwindled already to just over two thousand. Still, she was a courageous captain and death could not daunt her—it was, after all, part of the risk and thrill of war; the game of life and death that had made her scorn all other games as pretenses of life and adventure. And here she was, leading thousands of soldiers, even though they had dwindled by hundreds, and continuing to inspire them with deeds of true valor and gallantry. She lived for the fight, for the sweet smell of victory, for the succor of revenge. The city of Gaunt was besieged by her and her men. She had just to make them last another day and they would be there—staring their goal in the face.

In her exhilaration, she hardly slept at all. If only, she thought, if only she knew more of the strategies of war. For they were a little like the wiles and guiles of womenfolk. Games, she realized at that moment, that were played for survival with lives as the stake. There was nothing petty anymore about the extra penny for the red ribbon or the piece of lace; the charming of men and the admissions of inferiority. These were means of survival, tokens of success, rare touches of beauty in the otherwise bleak and unrelenting landscape of their lives. Fighting men were taught to play tricks and learn maneuvres and arraign men in battle lines in just the same way. But all Mary knew was the passion to win, the fearlessness to face any foe, and the daring to drive away the dread of even the weakest of her men.

By the time she had lain awake many hours, thinking of the sergeant-major, wondering what he would have done had he been alive, she knew she would not sleep at all. So she went instead to talk to the men on watch that night, then to check the supplies, assess how much powder they had left, how many bullets. For Mary knew tomorrow would be the day. And her mind was never once troubled by a doubt that they would win, only with questions of how they would win. With these thoughts in her mind she went to where the gunner lay, sleeping like a babe. The smell of muck, powder, and men's bodily secretions was powerful, and used as she was to the smells, Mary breathed deep through her mouth to minimize the stink in her nostrils.

She peered into the barrels. Empty! So many of them empty, yet standing there covered as if ready for battle! The bullets too were gone! Did the gunner know? Was he drugged? Had the Dutch somehow . . . ?

Out of the blue came the answer. He had been bought! Her most vital man and he had sold out to the enemy.

"How many men's lives for your miserable one?" she roared into the night. "How many of these brave men you sleep next to would lie slaughtered tomorrow if your deception had not been uncovered?"

The man shook so much his trousers were wet. The others around him awoke. Mary drew her sword.

"I'll make an end of you, you miserable traitor. You sell all England to save yourself."

"Stay a minute, Mary Ambree," pleaded a wise old soldier. "Give the gunner a chance to explain himself."

But Mary knew from that unerring womanly instinct that had come alive within her and guided her directly to the truth, she knew that the gunner had sent away her powder and her guns. Respecting the old man's hand on her arm, she asked the gunner to speak for himself. But he was a dithering, quavering jelly and could only mutter, "Spare me, Mary Ambree, spare me, spare me, spare me."

"Spare you when you single-handedly plotted to kill two thousand faithful men? Never."

And in the blinking of an eye she had drawn her sword and now held it high above the squatting man, vertical for a moment before it swooped down, dispensing justice, swift and steely. To the men looking on, Mary suddenly appeared a giantess. She seemed to grow bigger than ever before and her sword glinted and flashed with every breath she heaved from her giant body.

"One for your evil thoughts," she bellowed, and she cut off his head. It rolled from his neck and lay by his feet, gaping.

"The second for your pernicious heart." And she smote him in the chest. There was blood spurting. Blood, blood everywhere.

"And lastly for the belly that bred your treachery." And she slashed him in the belly with such ferocity that his body lay cut in three parts.

Then she turned and without a word she walked to battle.

Perhaps it was the anger burning in her. The despair that the enemy had what rightly belonged to her and her men. The thought that they believed they had the edge on her, that her men were leaving her. That the Dutch knew an Englishman would sell his compatriots while his captain lay in his makeshift bed, so feckless and reckless that he would approach such a crucial day without checking his strategies. Perhaps, she thought, they knew England was led by a lass and that's what gave them reason to scorn. For she saw a leer on every Dutchman's face that day and she killed him to transform it into a grimace. Perhaps it was because of all this that Mary Ambree demanded her men's everything in that battle. And perhaps that was why they fought as one massive force, driving themselves through colonnades of Dutchmen into the heart of Gaunt until they occupied the castle.

"Castle Gaunt is ours!" bawled Mary, her voice so raw from shouting and the smoke of gunpowder that she sounded like the rest of them. "Well done, men. Sleep easy. Tomorrow we begin defending our castle."

Oh, how they reveled that night, celebrating with song and food and cheers. And Mary forbade her men nothing but the taking of women against their will. Even Dutch women. About that she was adamant.

The Dutch troops wasted no time. They surrounded the castle, pressing in from all sides. But though she was besieged by them, fighting from within a castle was very different from fighting on bare ground outside with no walls to protect you save makeshift ones you've built yourself. And how Mary fought to keep that castle and how she inspired her men to fight with her!

Rumors were rife outside the castle about the English captain nicknamed "Courageous" by the Dutch. Captain Courageous was a magical lad—just young, not skilled or trained in the great art of war, but guided, some said, by the hand of God, while others had it that it was the hand of Old Nick himself.

But whatever the source of the luck, he was a hero of the type that was encountered in ancient myths. Some remembered accounts of a maid who had lived and fought in Orleans against her own king some hundred or two years before. She had been burned as a witch. Yes, there were stories aplenty about Mary Ambree, but not one person smelled a breath of the truth in them. And Mary gloried in her secret. She was fulfilling her mission in life. She knew she was born to be a soldier, born to win glory for England, born to heroism. And never a day went by when she didn't thank the sergeant-major for his guidance and his support and for bequeathing her his mantle so that she could fulfill the mission to which she had been born. To fight for England and to fight as, men thought, only a man can.

She looked often at her body. The soldier's uniform was one with her skin. It had become molded to her. It never came off. Though since the taking of the castle, Mary often thought of those womanly plots and maneuvres and all the strategies that made for survival.

It was not long before the Dutch launched a more determined effort than ever before to regain the castle. They besieged her on every side. They swore to beat down the castle walls. Whoever this Captain Courageous was, wherever he came from, whatever protected him, they would defeat him, they would storm the castle and take him prisoner. Mary heard that there were bets and prizes and rewards on her person. The Dutch were fighting against *her*. Not just the band of gallant Englishers but *her*—Mary Ambree—England's legendary captain. Her men wanted to throw a cordon of protection around her, advised her to fight from behind and not show herself. But the thrill that was in Mary could not be hidden. That glow that had burst from her in moments of glory suddenly began to stay with her all the time, as if taunting the enemy, as if throwing out torments and challenges. As if saying "Here I am. Do you think you can get me? You scum! You losers!"

She became more and more convinced that she was invincible, for she had both man and woman in her and that made her soul so strong, her spirit so resolute that no man could defeat it. As she stood on the battlement, showering both insult and injury on the Dutch, she thought how to employ the subtle and flexible skills of her sex. Then, as her woman's mind found the strategy, she went to the very edge of the wall of the castle and called out a unique challenge:

"Send me three of your best captains," she bawled, "and I'll see them out."

Well, how the Dutch laughed—and laughed and laughed to see the lithe figure of the fabled English captain. Captain Courageous! A mere child!

"Why, he hasn't even sprouted a hair on his face yet!" laughed one.

"And his voice is the voice of a mere fledgling! Just on the crack and not even in the chest yet."

"Not taught a lesson yet," growled the third. "Let's teach it to him ourselves."

"But wait," laughed Number One. "You're a seasoned captain. Does he need you to oust him?"

"And how would it look," cautioned Number Two, "if you and I were to come back with a scrap of a soldier like him and admit it took the three of us to vanquish him?"

"Look at you," scoffed Number Three. "Has your pride already made you forget that this soldier whom we dismiss as a mere slip of a boy has already beaten us to the castle? He's earned himself the nickname of Courageous. Those victories were won hard. I've seen him in battle rip a man limb from limb with a mighty roar that shakes your soul and shakes it so hard that you cannot see or hear or think for a moment. His barbarity is immense. It is demonic. And it is where he gets his power."

They had heard tales, the others agreed, of the savagery and fiendish power of the boy. Without a doubt they should not accept his challenge lightly and since he had asked for three it would do dishonor to their own men not to allow three men to volunteer. For what, otherwise, would people say except that the Dutch could not yield up three men among them who had the heart and the valor to face up to the wily and vicious Captain Courageous.

So, Number Three having carried the day, they advanced toward the castle and asked to be let in. Mary's men admitted the three Dutch captains and led them to Mary Ambree. Mary drew herself to her full height, lissome and tall and supple and covered all in smoke and grime but not so much as she had been in the days before they had taken the castle. For if there was one thing Mary most enjoyed, it was to wash herself and watch the dirt of the day pour away. But water was becoming scarce and the means to get more unlikely, so she rationed herself and could become only half as clean as she would have liked. And since the clothes were now one with her skin, she washed them and her body with the same strokes.

The captains saw Mary's face. It glowed through the grit and the soot and they were convinced in themselves now that she was no ordinary man and they were relieved that they were three and not one. Mary's men stood around, grim and gray and glaring.

Mary knew in a flash that she would not best these three

men. They were experienced swordsmen. First-rate fighters, brave, able, brawny. And she laughed inside herself as she knew that her plan would work wonderfully. Though such knowledge serves really only to make the thinker stand precariously on the razor's edge, enduring the risk and pain of being cut for the thrill of a possibility. No, you can never know for sure the outcome of such matters. But Mary decided to put her plan, forthwith, into action.

"Why, who do you think me or take me to be?" she asked with cheery daring.

The men hesitated. They had not expected to engage in talk, other than to determine the rules of the fight.

They growled and grimaced and grumbled a moment, then Number Three, nudged by the others, spoke up.

"A knight sir of England," he muttered, "and captain."

Mary threw back her head and laughed.

"And one who we mean to take away as our prisoner shortly," blurted out Number Two, incensed. How had the sprout expected them to answer? He was playing with them and would regret it. He had played with them like the jackal played with other animals and they had no time for wiles and wit—women's talents—and soldiers had no patience with them.

Mary laughed again and her scorn was plain.

"We are here to fight," snarled Number One. "Do us the courtesy of deciding on the rules of combat."

"So you mean to fight me, do you?" Mary's eyes narrowed, her voice was threateningly quiet and somber.

Suddenly Number Three remembered her horrendous bellow on the battlefield and felt a tremor in his knees.

"At your invitation," Number One retorted scornfully. "Else we would have taken you in our own way."

"I believe," said Mary, "that you and your men are of-fered rewards for capturing me?"

"We are not here for any rewards," snapped Number Three. "We're here in answer to your challenge. Now let us get on. We are fighting men, not prattlers. Talk, idle chatter, is for women among us Dutch. But we see that English soldiers prefer to talk."

There was a scuffling and a clanking as Mary's men moved forward provoked by the words. But she raised her hand.

"Let the Dutch speak," she ordered sternly, "for they are our guests."

Then once again she turned to the Dutch captains.

"So you think I'm a knight, a peer, and an English cap-tain?"

They spat, together, as if someone had given them a stage cue.

"Do you?" Mary insisted.

They nodded.

"That's what we said," conceded Number Three. "Now, when do we start fighting?"

"You consider it honorable to fight me?" she persisted.

"We would not be here else," they snapped, reaching for their swords.

"No captain of England, nor knight sir," said she trium-phantly, ripping off her jacket. "Behold! Two breasts in one bosom and therefore no knight! But only a poor, bonny lass, Mary Ambree."

The pain of ripping off that second skin was like burning in hell, but how Mary Ambree laughed! How she laughed and laughed to see the faces of those brave Dutch captains, their minds in disarray, jaws dropping to their chest, eyes fixed to her heaving, frolicking breasts. And she ran with the thoughts that raced in their minds: *"How will we deal with this?" "What will we tell our men?" "Are we to admit we've been bested by a woman?" "That we've dedicated time and fortune to fighting a mere girl?" "And do we now fight her in single combat? A poor lass, as she claims to be, and not a nobleman skilled in the virtuous arts of war?" "The disgrace would be too much."*

Number One and Number Two nudged Number Three, who blurted out his question immediately like a valiant gun spurting out the last of its powder on the depression of a trigger.

"But are you really a woman as you declare?"

"And has a woman made us spend our armor in war in this manner?" added Number One.

"We never saw the like of you in our lives!" exclaimed Number Two.

Mary removed her hat and took a deep bow. Her hair tumbled over her breasts, free and unbound now, the jacket flapping loosely about her like so much dead skin, flayed from her and hanging.

"At your service, gentlemen, and awaiting your decision to fight some more or not."

The three men blanched.

"As we said before," mumbled Number Three, "you are a miracle! No one has ever seen the like. So rather than fight you, Mary Ambree, we would honor you."

When they had left—and how they scuttled and pushed to get out of her sight—Mary breathed deeply. Her plan had worked. Being a woman was sometimes as useful in war as being a man. How glad she was to realize that.

And Mary laughed, a glad, throaty woman's laugh. And as she laughed, all the men in the castle gathered around her and hearing the tale from those present, they laughed too. The sound of near two thousand men laughing is a happy one and the castle shook with mirth that day!

And in the days that followed, the story of the triumph of Mary Ambree spread. Not everyone believed it to be anything more than the idle mythologizing of people incapable of accepting their defeat. But eventually the story reached the ears of Alexander Farnese, the Prince of Parma and the instigator of the siege.

Well, at first, like other educated men, he dismissed the rumor for what he thought it was—idle story-making. The Dutch were losing, so they made excuses of a woman in men's clothing and three captains so valiant that they withdrew from a chance of besting her and honored her instead. But then, as the tale accosted him everywhere he went, he decided to investigate it more thoroughly. And what did he find but that it was no story at all. It was the truth!

Now, the Prince of Parma had a secret longing to rule England along with everything else he had.

"If young Mary Ambree is nothing but a poor lass, she will surely be flattered by an offer of marriage from me. Nor will such an offer disgrace me, since she has excelled in war by winning me Gaunt."

So he sent her a glove of leather so soft that it was like silk, embroidered all in gold and studded with precious gems, and a diamond ring on a satin cushion, that sparkled and flashed as if there were within it a fiery white light, snatched from the burning bush even as the voice of God spoke to Moses.

And the emissary who brought the gifts to Mary conveyed the message to her immediately.

"The Prince of Great Parma has heard of your renown,"

he intoned, "and has wishes for alliance with fair England's crown. He therefore asks that you accept his invitation of marriage."

Mary stood up haughtily, stamped her foot, and tossed the hair off her face.

"Why! What do you think me or take me to be?" she demanded. "Though he is a prince and of great dignity, it shall never be said in my free, free England that a stranger married with Mary Ambree."

And Mary got to thinking about England and she thought a lot about it in the days that followed and decided that she wanted to go back again and breathe the air of which she was born. Nor, on the way back, did she think for a moment that she had given up the chance to become royalty, for she still held the foes of England in scorn and nothing, nothing, would ever make her forget the sergeant-major. The only man she ever had or ever would love. If there was another man born who could accept the spirit of a warrior in a woman, he was not likely to be born in Mary's time.

And so Mary decided to live a spinster and enjoy the honor that was heaped upon her. And how she spun and how she wove in the days that followed! Though it was not cloth she worked with but the fabric of life. She spun stories and she wove tapestries of words depicting worlds of love and of war, of loss and of victory, of accepting and of forsaking. For tale-making, after all, is the art of women.

THE MOUSE, THE
THING, AND THE WAND

But why am I different from other boys, Mother?"

"How are you different from other boys, child?"

"They've got a lump just here, Mother, like a mouse."

"Like a mouse?"

Mother repeats the child's words, partly from surprise, partly so that she has time to think. Should she tell, should she not?

"Well," explains the child, "sometimes it crouches quietly, out of sight, sometimes it gets up and plays. I haven't got a mouse."

"What does it matter if you don't have a mouse?"

"It makes me different."

"Different? Different from who?"

"From the other boys. They say it's because I'm a Muslim."

"What has your religion to do with anything?"

"Well, they say Muslims lop the mice off their boys as soon as they're born. So they call me Loppy." The child considers a moment. "Really, when they talk about Loppies, they mean all Muslims. But I'm the only one they know, so they call me Loppy."

"They don't lop it off," contradicts the widow, indignant. "They make a nick in it and take off the flapping skin on the end."

"Why?"

"To stop it flopping about and gathering dirt."

"Why don't the other tribes do it?"

"I think some do. And there are others—in faraway countries, I think they're called Yehudis—who do it too. Clean people do it. Don't you remember, old Ogedei telling stories around the fire of a long-ago khan who could change a staff into a snake? Don't you remember, he was put in a basket and sailed down a river far away from here—the Onan maybe, in the far part of the steppe. That man told them to do it—long ago. It's called circumcision. It is good to take that flap away, he said, for the sake of cleanliness and manliness and godliness."

"So why did you cut off all of mine?"

The old widow curses. Questions, questions, questions. If she was still living in a tent among her people of the Golden Horde instead of this heathen settlement, her child would not have to suffer such indignities. But then, of course, there would be other problems—ones she had left behind to come and live on a fixed plot of land in a house made from solid materials instead of the white felt tents fitted over their trellised wooden supports. Sedentary living had its advantages, particularly for women on their own, and she must take the good with the bad. She may not be in the heart of the steppe with the others, but she's just on the edge, after all, and close enough to join in the festivals to make sure her child grows up knowing about the beliefs and customs of the Golden Horde. The other women tease her a little about having become a "settler" but she counters their teasing by reminding them that the khans themselves have built cities and live in palaces. She knows the tribespeople are a little derisive about these city-dwellers—they have nicknames for them that suggest they have become "soft." Still, that's nothing to this latest problem, which has been simmering since the moment she became a mother. She and the child have a lot of suffering to endure in the days to come.

She looks at the child's face. Quite radiant. Children take things in their stride so easily. A mother would probably suffer a week for what her child had been through while the child whistled it away in a moment. Puff! Blown away! Gone in a single gesture. In the end, what was better—to dismiss life's hardships as mere trivia or allow them to weigh you down? The first may be more enticing but the second was the right way. Why was the hard way always the proper one; the easy one, the enjoyable one, always the path to sin? She often wondered if children were meant to make life easier or more difficult. People said they were a blessing. But people said a lot of things and she couldn't believe them all.

She looked at the child's luminous face. He? She? She often forgot herself, about Rahat. She'd given him a unisex name. Ecstasy, it meant. Ecstasy. What an irony! And here she was again. *Him*, she had said. Well, the river had run toward its source since the day she'd given birth instead of away from it, that was for sure. For the child was born a girl.

"A girl for a widow is no wonderful thing," she explains grumpily. "Who will support me in my old age? Who will help me get the outside work done? I reared you as a boy because it will give you greater freedom. See how you can play with the children outside while the daughters around are all cramped indoors and let out only to draw water or carry firewood. You have no mouse because you were born a girl."

She rants and raves about the terrible lot of women, and Loppy can't deny that most of what she says is true. How the women around her toil and labor and break their backs—or have them broken for them by the menfolk. If being a woman means drawing water from the well and never riding and always taking the blame and growing wizened and cracked and embittered, then she is relieved not to be a woman. Loppy does not feel deprived about not having a mouse. She has no idea what they are good for anyway except to urinate with. She is used to her own mechanism, which is more satisfactory to use while squatting. If she stands, the warm liquid runs down the sides of her legs, turning cold and itchy, and the stains it leaves on her britches acquire a stench as they dry. The mouse is easy to use standing up. It grows long and the boys position it well away from where they stand and squirt it free so that nothing splashes back onto them. She lets the boys think hers was cut off when she was born.

"And I'll say the same thing to my wife when you grow old and I marry to relieve you of your work," Loppy tells her mother.

"Why get married anyway?" mutters the old woman. She has always dreaded the problems that youth will bring. And youth comes as fast as it goes, so she is always wary, always on the watch. "What does marriage ever give you but children? Unhappiness, problems, responsibility."

There goes Mother again. Loppy goes out to play. She enjoys her games with the other boys. They test who can stay longest on horseback without being tied on. The boys who are not riding watch the girls outside their makeshift houses. They have become very interested in them lately. They fantasize about touching them and lying down beside them or showing them their mouse and getting them to stroke it. Loppy finds their conversation disgusting, but she keeps quiet trying to think how it would be to live like a girl. Do they ever play? she wonders. Could she be one of them? She shakes her head. No, never. Some of them have humps growing on them—on their chests instead of their backs. They look ugly. Rahat shudders. She was never meant to be one of them. That's why her mother brought her up as a boy. That's why her name means ecstasy. That's why she hasn't got the humps on her chest. She makes her way home, thinking about the humps and bumps she hasn't got—none between her legs, none on her chest—and realizes that her mother has those bumps on her chest too, although they are not all hard and thrusting like those of the girls but soft and sagging like a hill returning to the plain. It strikes her that as a baby she was probably suckled on them. Of course! That is what they are for—to feed babies, after growing them first. She shudders at the thought of an alien being spreading inside her, then leeching on her body like a limpet. It reminds her of possession. Or a ghoul or vampire, sucking out her liquid. No. Far better to be a man, even if her mouse is missing.

Repugnant thoughts enshroud her in a swirling mist of gray and she fills with anger, so that when she feels something moist and soft wrap itself around her fingers, she pulls away in disgust. When at last she makes herself look, she sees a girl. She must be about—what? Nine, ten? A year or two younger than herself, she thinks.

"Why did you grab my hand?" she demands.

"I'm lost."

Fancy, eh? The girl speaks with airs and graces. Her voice sounds of palaces, not the rugged steppes where Rahat lives. Her clothes speak too, in soft whispers.

"What are you doing here?" Rahat asks.

"I came with my father's entourage. I got separated from them."

"Entourage, eh?" Rahat grins. "Which horde do you belong to?"

"Horde?" The girl looks bewildered.

"Horde. You know, tribe, clan. Which people do you belong to?"

"I don't belong to any people," she replies in bewilderment. "People belong to me. My father is the supreme one."

Rahat is wonderstruck. Is this one of those Devs that the storytellers speak of, a sort of goddess? Her skin is translucent—as if the muck and dust do not dare to settle on it. Her hair is a dark shiny brown, not dull gold with dust and sun.

"Well, if he's that supreme, he'll find you, no doubt."

Rahat decides it would be safer to move out of this magical creature's orbit. But the ethereal creature bursts into tears when she walks on.

"Why are you crying?" Rahat asks in exasperation, peering carefully at her tears to see if there are gems among them. The storyteller says Devs weep precious jewels. "It's getting dark. I have to get home. I still have work to do."

"Can't I come with you?"

Rahat is worried. "Well, I'm not sure," she replies. "We're quite poor, really. I don't know if we've got food for a creature like you. And our home is okay but with you there it would probably look quite shabby. I mean, my mother may not have enough . . ."

"Oh, please take me with you," begs the girl, "I'm frightened and lonely. And when my father's men find me, you'll be well rewarded. My name is Eshka. It means loving."

"And my name is Rahat, which means ecstasy, but my friends call me Loppy because I'm a Muslim and—" She stops herself mid-flow. These are not matters for a boy to discuss with a girl. But then, she is not a boy and— She stops again. Do girls discuss such matters with other girls? she wonders. Eshka's interruption answers her question.

"I know what Loppy means," she giggles. "It's what the heathens call us Muslims. You must be a Muslim if they call you Loppy."

Loppy laughs. "So you know. They talk about these subjects where you live too, do they?"

"Of course. My maids are always going on about men's Thing. Sometimes the guards show them theirs. I've never seen a Thing. But I know all about it and how it works and what it does when it wakes up and gets angry."

Rahat assumes an air of nonchalance, gratified to see from the corner of her eye that Eshka has mistaken it for embarrassment and turned an amusing shade of red. She has learned a bit more about the mouse from Eshka, which is an unexpected bonus, because now she can participate more with the others when they talk about theirs. Which they increasingly do.

The old woman grumbles to herself when she sees them coming.

"What is this you've brought with you?" she snarls.

"A visitor, Mother. She's lost and has to stay until her father's men find her."

"So who's stopping her?" replies the old woman. She is a Muslim, after all, and they have their rules of hospitality. Their Prophet would have given his only date and his last drop of honey or milk to a visitor. And as for the roof over their head. Well, they were not only obliged by the code to share it with any visitor who asked, but they were to make the visitor feel they were happy to do it. She embraces Eshka and invites her to sit down at the table, realizing that she is not welcoming this little girl because of any code of behavior but from the impulse in her heart. "And what a fine and beautiful girl you look too."

Rahat notices a tear glinting in her mother's eye.

"Why are you crying, Mother?" she demands.

"Oh, nothing," the old widow replies, brushing away the dew from her cheek. "Just that I bore a daughter once—but I reared a son. And every day of the week I miss my daughter and wonder what she would have been like if I'd been able to keep her. But you are a wonderful son to me, Rahat, and I wouldn't be without you for a hundred daughters. Still, Eshka brought back old thoughts. A woman's lot is hard, you know. Your heart is made of cotton flowers and you have to treat it like steel. But God has sent me Eshka so that I can have a taste of the pleasures of a daughter for a while."

So Eshka is made welcome and seems contented enough. Rahat is flattered by all the attention she focuses upon her and plays less with the boys, more with Eshka. Perhaps this is because it's the first time she has ever known a girl. The old woman grows hawk eyes, she seems to scrutinize everything they do. She mutters dark warnings to Rahat, who says Eshka worships her as one worships a savior. The old woman likes it best when Eshka is safe with her, helping her around the house. Eshka does not fuss about the quite ordinary style of life she has to live and helps as much as she can. Rahat and the old woman learn not to question the strange words that she sometimes comes out with such as "Father will be pleased to know I have learned the ways of the people," "I have never drunk koumiss before." What hordeswoman doesn't know about koumiss, when they ferment it year in, year out, milking the mares, creating the whey, before finally storing away the mixture to drink on festival days. Once or twice Eshka even gives the impression that in her former life she never had to work, or even walk. Did she perform her work by magic? Did she fly? They do not even wonder about it anymore.

Eshka and Rahat grow closer every day.

"Will you come and live with me and my father?" she murmurs, stroking Rahat's cheek.

The old woman overhears and is beside them in a shot.

"What is this talk of leaving an old widow and going to live elsewhere?" she demands. For the rest of the day she buzzes around Rahat, trying to catch her alone.

"I become anxious," she reprimands Rahat when they are finally on their own, "when you talk to Eshka that way. You know you are a woman and she does not. You must forbid her to behave that way."

"Which way exactly, Mother?" asks Rahat. She is innocent, not canny in the ways of women like Eshka.

"You must not let her touch you," Mother commands.

"You are both women. If she finds out you have been deceiving her, she will be devastated. No touching."

"But I love her, Mother," says Rahat simply, "and she says she loves me. We want to be married."

The old woman lets out a bloodcurdling howl and beats her head.

"That can never be! Never! Never!"

"Calm down, Mother, please, please calm down," implores Rahat, misunderstanding the old woman's consternation. "I promise not to go away and leave you alone. I will never abandon you."

Eshka appears, to investigate the noise. The old woman says the crisis is over.

"Your brother," she says pointedly, indicating Rahat, "your brother is my only means of support. He has earned our bread since he was seven. I could not live without him. And what a wonderful sister you have been to him. My two children—so wonderful—how I'm blessed."

"If you refer to your spouse as a sibling," she mutters darkly to Rahat afterward, "your marriage is abrogated out of hand. You see how strong a bond is that one? So never, never again think of marrying that girl. She is your sister. It would be a sin. There was a woman once—Fatima—a companion and confidante of Turkina, Khan Batu's stepmother. The khan pronounced her a witch and when she confessed, her genital orifices were sewn up and she was cast into the river. Do you know why they sewed up those parts in particular? Because everyone knows witches love other women as men love their wives. It is the quickest way of determining a witch. Be warned."

Rahat and Eshka joke a little about the old woman's fear of being left alone, but underneath it all Rahat is anxious. The days go by and she tries to do as the other boys do and flirt with other girls. But she cannot. She loves only Eshka. Eshka knows so much more about the bodies of men and women than she does. Sometimes she longs to tell her she is a girl too, so that Eshka can teach her how girls feel and tell her, from the information she has gathered in her father's home, how the bodies of men behave and how they feel and what they want. And then she can examine her own strange and new impulses and urges— inexplicable desires that feel much the same as the longings the boys describe.

"Would Eshka really be devastated if I told her I've lied about being a boy?" she wonders. "After all, it's only half a lie because, apart from the missing mouse, I'm really no different from them."

Nevertheless, when Eshka asks in a saucy mood one day if Rahat will show her his Thing, she refuses indignantly.

"Not now," she mumbles. "Not until we are married."

"How prim and proper." Eshka pouts.

It is the first time Rahat has regretted not having a Thing. Distraught, she wanders into the steppes, staring at the sky, thinking about the mockery her body is making of her. She strokes her cheeks, longing for the straggly growth appearing on the faces of her friends. She is nearly fourteen, with neither breast nor beard. She looks deep into herself and spies the soul of a young man. She can see herself, a young man in a woman-shaped cage, waiting, longing, for a large stallion on which to fly to freedom. And at that moment something her mother often says comes miraculously true. "Make your wishes carefully," Mother always says. "Because there's a wishing hour, a moment of acceptance and no one knows when that may come." A large black horse, approaching at a swift gallop, whispers in her ear and even before his rider notices, flies on, leaving Rahat puzzling over its message.

"When the time comes, demand me for your reward."

"Strange," she thinks. "What can that mean?"

But it must be time to go back to habitation if she believes horses talk.

She wanders home and discovers that the rider of the horse came with a message from the khan of the empire. His daughter is lost: if anyone has news, they should inform his messenger.

"I suppose," says the old woman, resigned, "that our idyll is over. I have asked Eshka and she has confessed she is the daughter of the khan. Take her back to the palace, Rahat, and return her to her mother and her father."

The old woman packs enough food and drink for the journey and says a tender good-bye to Eshka. She wishes Rahat a safe return and watches with tears in her eyes until they turn into a puff of dust in the distance.

The khan's capital is far but not as far from their settlement as they have always thought, and as they enter the city gates the guards recognize Eshka and there is immediate celebration. Huge kettledrums throb like the first heartbeat of Creation. Spontaneously, the townspeople emerge from their houses with gifts of flowers and food and drink. Women let out throaty trills of jubilation and the khan himself rides out on a lithe and glossy black horse that whisks its mane and swishes its tail and tosses its head like a wave ornamenting the sea, serving no one's will but its own. And the horse fixes its great brown eyes on Rahat and she hears its whispering in her mind.

"Choose me," it commands, *"when the khan offers you a reward."*

"Well," says the khan after he has embraced his daughter and thanked Rahat many times for restoring her to the kingdom. "You must come to the palace and join our feast. Then, when you have seen all the splendors of the city, you may have what you like. I will refuse you nothing—absolutely nothing but my crown because I am only its temporary guardian and it is God's and not mine to give."

So Rahat and Eshka accompany the khan to his palace, where she is immediately whisked away to meet her mother and then sent to her apartments and massaged and perfumed and pampered in the way that princesses are meant to be. Rahat wanders around the palace and the city, bewildered by her surroundings and overwhelmed by the retinue assigned to entertain her. At last it is time for the night meal and they all meet again.

Rahat does not have a chance to speak to Eshka, but their eyes meet and she can see Eshka and feels better for it. They feast among courtiers and the khan and other important men make speeches and give and receive gifts for the safe return of Princess Eshka. Rahat is a little sad throughout the ceremony. She knows it is not long before it will all come to an end and she has to return laden with gifts but empty inside, to her settlement and her mother. And she will never see Eshka again.

"If I were a woman," she thinks miserably, "I could be her servant and live with her and serve her all my life. But I do not have a woman's heart. And to pretend otherwise would be like denying the truth. No, I would rather pay the price of my convictions."

She remembers her mother's words and speculates whether Turkina's maid felt the same before she was tortured and drowned for a witch.

Looking over at Eshka's face, luminous and dewy as the full moon, she is plunged into darkness knowing that she will soon revolve out of her orbit.

"And Eshka?" she speculates. "Beautiful, vital Eshka with your sharp, knowing mind and your impetuous ways, will you remember the peasant boy from the steppe and spare a memory for the love you once felt for him, I wonder?"

But Eshka, far and away and on the other side of the long table beside her mother, the queen, glows and shines and smiles at Rahat, oblivious of her anguished thoughts, just as the moon is impervious to the suffering of the people upon whom she casts her radiance.

The khan draws the feast to a close and rises to thank Rahat formally.

"If he is an example of our steppesmen," he states, "then we have nothing to fear from our enemies and a great deal to be proud of about ourselves. And before I bring tonight's celebrations to a close, Rahat—my daughter's savior—ask for your reward. I will refuse you nothing."

Rahat stands.

"Your Majesty," she begins, "I am used to the hardships of the steppe, though I live a sedentary life. But since I have been in your kingdom I have seen wonder after wonder, things that are beautiful beyond imagination: fabrics and treasures and riches that old men tell about in tales around the fire at night, of days when the hordes of the Great Khans visited countries in the western world and saw people with transparent skins. They say these people had hair of spun gold and blazing fire; their eyes were the color of the sky and the forest and they spoke in strange tongues and had exotic customs. We boys often argued how much of this came from the imagination of the storyteller.

Now, I know more wonderful things exist than the fancy of people could ever conjure up. And when I tell my people what I have seen, they'll wonder which parts of my story are real and which from the world of make-believe. Knowing they are true is more than anyone could ever ask."

There is silence as Rahat pauses, swallowing back her tears. And into the sad silence rushes a whispering sound.

"Choose me!" And before Rahat has time to collect her thoughts the words rush from her mouth like a glossy black horse, whisking its mane and swishing its tail. "A horse is always valuable to a steppesman. Your generous words have made me bold, so I ask for the black horse that you rode this morning. It acquitted itself well in our tough and treacherous terrain when it carried your messenger there in search of the princess. Will you give me that horse?"

A terrified hush falls over the table.

"The black mare?" echoes the khan, flabbergasted. "You want the black mare?"

"I do," confirms Rahat unhappily, sensing she has done wrong.

"But she is the best horse in the world. She is worth my entire kingdom," declares the khan, shaking in his effort to conceal his fury. At last he speaks again. "Well, if you must have her, you must have her. But you might just as well have my daughter too. Because I love that animal as much as I love my own child. Besides, I believe that you should give your daughter to someone beneath her and a man to someone above. Such partnerships bring harmony to the people."

Rahat's heart leaps in jubilation. She looks across the table and Eshka looks back at her, smiling, her eyes deeply inviting. Rahat nods her assent, unable to speak. The khan and queen note the loving exchange, and a great cheer rises around the table. A wedding date is set and soon Rahat and Eshka are married amid great rejoicing and splendor.

In the wedding chamber, all decorated with garlands and pearls and perfumed with oils and spices, Eshka and Rahat talk and joke and tease and caress. Finally they undress, stroking each other with increasing urgency in the magical torchlight that flickers and waves, registering every breath.

"Don't be so mean, Rahat," pouts Eshka. "Show me your Thing. We're married now."

"I haven't got a Thing," replies Rahat, laughing. "Don't you remember, that's why the boys at home call me Loppy?"

"You think I'm ignorant," squeals Eshka. "Well, I'm not, you know. Nothing is private in a palace. For every hundred women longing to pass on their secrets, another hundred are longing to find out. So I probably know more about these things than you ever will."

"That's probably true, Eshka," replies Rahat humbly, "because you're a princess and I'm only a peasant. But I am the one they call Loppy and it's because I've been circumcised."

"Well then," continues Eshka, not believing a word, "there's only one way to prove you've been cut so savagely. I'll have to see for myself."

She lifts a torch out of its holder and brings it down to Rahat's body and the next moment she has discovered the truth.

"You're not a man at all," she gasps. "You're a woman. Why did you deceive me like this?"

"I didn't deceive you," replies Rahat, alarmed. "I didn't. I am a boy in every sense of the word. I just don't have a mouse."

"You disgust me," shrieks Eshka. "You've been cheating

me all these months. You've played with my feelings and I hate you. Get out of my chamber. Get out of my sight."

"Please listen to me, Eshka," pleads poor Rahat. "Let me explain how I feel."

But Eshka goes storming out of the chamber to her father and in the morning the khan summons Rahat. Distraught and exhausted after her sleepless night, Rahat stands miserably in the presence of the khan. He is bound to reprimand her, put her to death even. Like Turkina's friend. But what does she care? She wants to die anyway, as long as it is not like that poor woman with her orifices stitched together and drowned in the Oxus. Life has become too twisted to imagine, even more incredible than the stories of old men around campfires.

"My mother bore a daughter," she thinks, "but reared a son. A woman marries a woman and mares talk. What terrible confusion!"

The khan breaks into her thoughts. "Since you have taken my beloved mare for yourself," he says angrily, "I want you to go and fetch me her brother."

Rahat agrees and without considering what she has agreed to, she makes her way out to the black mare.

"My mother bore a daughter," she tells the mare, "but reared a son. A woman marries a woman and a mare talks."

The mare throws back her head and laughs, rearing her forelegs in amusement.

"Not only do I talk," she whinnies, "but I see into the future. Tell me, why do you think I entered your story?"

"What story?" splutters Rahat, bewildered.

"Your own amazing story," replies the mare. "But tell me first, what is its opening chapter? What has the khan asked you to do?"

"Well," says Rahat, "he wants me to find your brother and I don't know where and I don't know how. I'm just an illiterate peasant."

"But I'm a magic mare and I'm telling you that you have to watch out for that wily khan. He's sending you on this mission so that you will die and no one will ever know he killed you."

"Ah," sighs Rahat. "Well, that will suit me fine, because I want to die."

"And why's that?"

"Because God locked a boy in a girl's body and I no longer want to live a life of imprisonment."

"Tush!" snorts the mare. "You're giving up before even trying. How will you know the end of the story if you're not even willing to allow the Great Storyteller to tell it first? When you sit around the campfire at home, listening to tales, you don't jump up at every pause and shout that you won't stay, for this bit or that bit is impossible. No! You go with him where he takes you and in the end everything comes together according to the Great Plan of life. Then you can decide whether you like the tale or not."

The mare instructs Rahat to return to the khan and ask him for a keg of old wine.

"Take two," says the khan, thinking it well worth the price of two kegs of old wine to get rid of this dreadful travesty of his sex—a woman who thinks she is a man. The thought makes him shudder.

"One's enough," replies Rahat, and hoisting the keg easily over her shoulder, returns to the stables.

"Saddle me up and we'll leave at once," says the mare. "Saddle me up and get on my back and I'll take you to my brother. He is a sea horse and we need to make our way to the stretch of the Aral Sea where he lives."

"I don't need to scar your back with a saddle!" laughs Rahat, leaping onto the mare's back. "I'm a child of the Golden Horde. I know how to shape my body to fit my horse. Now take me to your brother as fast as you can."

The mare throws back her head and whinnies. "On my head and my eyes, child of the Golden Horde, I'll carry you through all the stops to the end of your story."

Rahat is touched by the mare's expression—only her mother has ever used it to her before. It means the mare puts her before anything. *On my eyes and on my head.* Rahat used to say it to Eshka but Eshka no longer values anything Rahat can offer. She has colluded with her father in sending her to her death.

"My life is a travesty," she mourns. "My mother thought that she could improve our lives by dressing me as a man. But God seems to have put an enduring curse on all women— whether they dress in men's clothing or their own, they bear a burden of suffering. None of this would have happened to me if I had not been born a woman."

"I feel you growing heavier," the mare complains, slowing down. "It is because you are grieving. Lighten your heart. It will be easier on my back and we will get there quicker. Remember, I have entered your story to make your burden lighter on the road that leads to the achievement of your desires."

"I know, my faithful mare, I know," weeps Rahat. "And I promise to try."

Well, the mare flies, swift as the wind over desert and over forest, over land and over sea, over river and over mountain until at last she comes to land on a long stretch of beach, near a raging silver sea.

Rahat shivers with cold and shudders with fear as the mare lands and canters along the shore looking around before finally coming to a stop by an old stone fountain.

"Dismount, Rahat," she says, "and pull the plug from the fountain. When the water has run out, plug the hole again and fill the pond with your keg of wine. My brother, the sea horse, will smell the wine and come ashore to drink it. He is not used to wine and it will make him light-headed. Take your chance then and catch hold of him. My brother is as swift as I am and more powerful. Hold fast to his mane as he begins to run and tell him his sister is waiting for him by the fountain."

Rahat listens carefully, crouching in the shadows behind the fountain, waiting for the sea horse to come. And here he comes, magnificent as the sea, tail whirling, eyes blazing, skittish, and full of the capricious wrath of the sea in a storm. He throws back his head, breathes deeply, then steadies up and makes his way to the fountain, where he drops his muzzle and drinks deeply until all the wine is gone, every last drop. Then he steps back, reeling a little, and Rahat darts forward and grabs a portion of his mane.

Just as the mare warned, the great white stallion charges forward, but Rahat is prepared. She keeps a firm hold on him, shouting her message.

"Ho! Ho! Wait! I have a message from your sister, the black mare. She's waiting for you by the fountain."

The horse slows down. His sister comes running up to him and the two greet each other and speak in their language. The mare tells her brother Rahat's sad story and begs him not to let her young mistress go to the execution block. Finally the stallion is persuaded to go back with them. Once he has agreed, they hurry back as swiftly as they came.

Back at the palace, Rahat requests an audience with the khan and presents him with the sea horse. Then, begging his leave, she returns to see her beloved Eshka.

"Why have you come back?" demands Eshka. "Has some miracle transformed you into a man?"

Rahat drops her eyes. "No, I am the same Rahat you once loved. I haven't changed."

At these words Eshka storms out of the room cursing her father and vowing that she will not rest until Rahat has been punished severely for her deception.

"What you have done," she remonstrates, "is evil in the eyes of God and humankind."

When she has left, Rahat cries. Her limbs are sore and so is her heart, but she has no time to rest because the khan summons her to court.

"I have a job for you," he growls. "The imps of the gold mines have not paid me their dues for three years. Collect them before nightfall tomorrow."

Wearily, Rahat goes to her black mare.

"We have another journey to make," she says, explaining the new mission. "Rest tonight, but we'll leave tomorrow at the break of dawn."

"Rest?" snorts the mare. "I don't need a rest. Let's go now. Why waste time?"

So Rahat leaps onto the mare's back and off they go, swift as the wind, across forests and deserts, rivers and mountains and finally into a deep, hidden valley to the Mansion of Imps. In their mansion, the imps are feasting and drinking after a long day's work in the mines.

"Go in," commands the mare, "and tell them the khan's armies are seizing the gold mines because the imps haven't paid their tithes. The imps will run out to defend the mines. When you are alone, take everything valuable you can find and leave immediately. I will be waiting here."

Rahat is frightened but she squares her shoulders, raises her chin, and marches boldly into the Mansion of Imps.

"Oh!" chortle some of the imps as she enters. "A delectable little tidbit has walked in. I saw him first, he's mine."

"Don't be greedy," sneers another, crawling off his chair and onto Rahat's foot. "There's plenty here for all of us. What a fine figure of a man."

"The kidneys for me," shrills one as they all crowd around.

"The brains for me," yells another, trying to sink his teeth into Rahat's skull.

"I wouldn't advise that," yells Rahat, plucking him out and throwing him down. "I am a madman and you may get madman's disease."

"I'm having the liver and the pancreas!" claims a third.

"I'm surprised you can think of your bulging tummies," Rahat says in a loud voice. "Can't you hear the Great Khan's army out there, seizing your mines and confiscating your gold because you won't pay your dues?"

In one glutinous mass the imps race from the room, jostling, shoving, climbing over each other until the room is clear and Rahat alone in it. Swiftly she glances around and sees a large leather bag on a bushel in the corner of the room. It is heavy with gold as she heaves it onto her shoulder and races out to the mare. The imps chase after her, shrieking and cursing, but Rahat leaps onto the mare's back. In a moment her blackness has merged with the night and they ride the wind back to the khan's capital.

"Your Majesty," pants Rahat when she returns at dawn, "here's enough gold to cover your taxes for the past three years and the next. Now, if you will permit me, I should like to bathe my tired limbs and rest for the night."

The khan is speechless.

"You are no wo . . . man," he splutters. "You're the very devil himself. Or how could you have done what an entire battalion could not?"

"I am no devil," protests Rahat, alarmed, "I am a dedicated Muslim—and now I am going to bathe and offer my thanks to God."

Back in the chamber she still shares with Eshka, Rahat immerses herself in a warm bath and washes away some of the exhaustion of her journey. Afterward, as she lies stretched out on the divan in the anteroom, she senses a shadow hovering over her and sits up with a shock. It is Eshka. Her eyes blaze and her voice is harsh as she demands once again: "Why have you come back? Has some miracle transformed you into a man?"

"No, I haven't changed. I am the same Rahat that you once loved. I stayed away from you because I know you hate me."

For a moment Eshka seems to relent.

"You made me promises you knew you could never keep," she whispers sadly. Then her rage returns and she storms out of the room cursing her father and vowing that she will not rest until Rahat has been severely punished for her deception.

"What you have done," she cries, "is evil in the eyes of God and humankind."

When she has left, Rahat weeps. It is true she had promised to make Eshka a good and loving husband. But she had not known then that Eshka would mind about the missing Thing. Now, having been so close to the desires and ecstasies of the wedding chamber, she realizes its function. She remembers that when the boys at home had used it they began calling it a wand. They said using it transformed them from boys to men.

"Well," she laments, "I have no wand so I can never turn into a man." And she lies down again and weeps. "Oh, God, grant the khan's wish and let me die."

She looks up at the intricately painted ceiling—blue to represent the heavens from the dome of the universal tent supported by the medial column of the pole star. From there, God casts down His radiance and His power. Rahat sees faint shafts of dawn light filter down on her through carefully created openings in the ceiling: nature perfectly reproduced in artifice.

"Do You favor men because they are in Your image?" she defiantly apostrophizes her Maker. "My mother and my wife would both have what they want if I had been a man. I am unhappy only because I am a woman. But if it is true that You love all Your creatures equally, woman or man, human or beast, beast or bird, then send me a sign. Give me the body of a man."

Rahat's prayer, if you can call it that, is interrupted by a summons from the Great Khan.

"I have a job for you," says the khan. "Bring me the rosary

of the great ogress who prays in the land beyond the sun. If you are not back by sunset, I will have your head."

As Rahat leaves the khan's chamber, she hears him give orders for her execution.

"He will never survive this ordeal," chortles the khan. "Then I'll be rid of him."

"This will be our last mission together, dear friend," Rahat confides in the mare. "Then I'll trouble you no more."

"What are you talking about?" demands the mare, impatient. "What trouble? Which mission?"

Rahat explains what the khan wants now, and the mare, as usual, reassures Rahat that the mission can be achieved.

"And no talk of endings and death," she commands firmly, "just to please me."

"On your head and your eyes, beloved ally," Rahat promises, "I'll try to keep up my spirits though you have to admit the Planner of Fate has played some strange tricks on me. You more than anyone know that my mother bore a daughter and reared a son, a woman married a woman and mares talk. Heaven knows what I'll add to that list before my story's told."

The mare flings back her head and whinnies and frolics in merriment as she takes off, and in the flick of Rahat's wrist they have arrived on a mountain peak. Rahat dismounts and looks around her. On the edge of a terrifying precipice, beneath an overhanging rock, sleeps an enormous woman.

"That is the mother ogress," explains the mare, "and there above her is the rosary—her most precious possession. She killed her sons for it, but you can steal it from her and get away. Now, listen carefully and do exactly as I say. When you see her attendants come out carrying the rosary on a silver platter, you will know it's time for her to wake up. Grab it just as she reaches for it, and run. It will take her a moment to realize what has happened. In that time you will be on my back and we'll be on our way."

Rahat feels full of courage. She has nothing to lose but her life, and if she cannot be Eshka's husband, she does not want to live anyway. But she has promised her mare that she will do her best so she stands by the rock, just behind the sleeping ogress, while the mare conceals herself in the dark crevices of the abyss. After a long, dreary wait a demoness appears carrying a silver platter bearing the rosary. As she approaches, the mother ogress clenches her eyes, yawns, and stretches out a hand for the rosary. At that moment Rahat darts forward, snatches the rosary, and races down toward the slopes where the black mare is waiting.

"Curse you!" shrieks the mother ogress. "I curse you for stealing my most treasured possession. If you are a woman, become a man. If a man, become a woman!"

Rahat leaps onto the back of the waiting mare and, as before, they flash off toward the khan's palace, swift as lightning.

Rahat shifts on her mount; she squirms—is this a mouse she feels in her trousers? She can hardly allow herself to believe that the ogress's curse has taken effect. She wriggles and wiggles and finally she is convinced. She has a Thing!

"A wand!" whinnies the mare, reading her thoughts. "That will change your life."

Well, this time when Rahat enters the khan's chamber he has a swagger about him, and a grin and a squareness to his shoulders that commands larger amounts of space around his body than ever before. He hands the rosary over to the khan and his voice rings out in deep, resonating tones, like his older playmates who had turned into men back on the steppe. And he notices that the khan is looking at him as if he notes some vital change.

"Now, sire," says Rahat, "I must go and rest because my limbs are weary and my wife is waiting."

The khan splutters and stutters as Rahat strides from the room enjoying his newly acquired aura of power.

"How strange," he thinks, "that when I was a woman I never enjoyed victory in quite the same way."

In his chambers he orders his bath to be drawn and calls to Eshka to prepare herself for him. He spends a long time immersing himself in the warmth of the bath before he eventually emerges and stalks into Eshka's bedchamber. He is draped in a large, soft sheet and stands confronting her with a challenging look on his face. Eshka sits crouched on her bed, not quite knowing what to expect. Rahat has never been so authoritative, so imperious, before. What, she wonders, is she going to do?

"Why have you come back?" she falters, and the old haughtiness is gone from her voice. "Has some miracle transformed you into a man?"

Rahat drops his gaze. "I am the same Rahat you once loved," he says firmly.

Eshka looks carefully at him. There is something about the way he speaks—his voice has changed. Not just the manly quality of it, but its tone and expression. It suggests a reassurance Rahat never had before.

"I still love you, Eshka," he says, "and you agreed to marry me in the presence of God and a million people. In full view and hearing of thousands, you told the *qadi*, not once, not twice, but three times, that you accepted me, Rahat, as your husband. Do you still love me? Are you prepared to fulfill the promise you made?''

Eshka leaps up to storm out of the room, cursing her father and vowing that she will not rest until Rahat has been punished severely for her deception. But Rahat steps forward and catches her by the arm.

"Don't go yet," he pleads. "I have something to show you."

He drops his sheet and stands before her in full naked splendor. Eshka's hands fly to her mouth.

"Oh, Rahat! A Thing! You've got one after all!"

"A wand, Eshka, a wand," replies Rahat proudly. "Because it will transform you from my enemy into my wife."

Amazed and delighted, Eshka leaves Rahat standing naked in the middle of the bedchamber and runs to her father to call off the execution.

"Rahat is a man after all," she exclaims, "I'm happy, Father. I love him and I don't want him killed."

Well, the khan is so relieved he changes the execution into a celebration and Eshka returns quickly to her room and throws herself into Rahat's arms.

Down in the stables the black mare tosses her mane, whisks her tail, and frolics in delight.

THE SAND-SIFTER

If you look out when dawn is turning into morn, you see a fine, barely visible veil between the two; it refines the light, mellows it. And if you reach out your hand to rent that veil, you get it back moist—rarely—but mostly with a coating of ground grit as tangible as fantasy.

I always feel that God is in that fantasy dust—in every atom of it as it billows in great golden waves, settling in sunshine dunes—on and on and on—and even farther into the pictures the eye creates and beyond into imagination. The desert defies the finite. It is grounded in the center of the universe and kisses the skies. You see it, you don't see it. It is alluring, the desert, but beware of choosing its path without devotion, because it can mete out a harsh and painful justice. And when you

come out of it, the dust clings, millions of littl[e]
your hair and nose, under your eyelids and nails
your throat, and all the minor and intimate crev[ices]
some of it descends into your heart.

I look down at myself, my hair cropped, my clothes
patched and faded, clutching my Bible—my only book—in this
small cell in Rome. My life and work have been in Rome for
some thirty years but it is my repudiated womanhood that reminds me today of the place in which I left it behind. And my
life folds in on me, beginning in Rome, ending in Rome, and in
the middle, Egypt—vast, rich, softly swelling gold, like the
smoothly curving mound of a woman with child. I can feel its
satiny touch on my fingers still, coating the pages of my books
in the library of my father, Philip, Prefect of the Roman Emperor.

It seems impossible I was ever a daughter of Rome. I see
myself again as I was in those days in Alexandria—clothed in
the finest of fabrics, living in a palace, surrounded by books.
The sand is on them too—sometimes shimmering, sometimes
filmy—but I've never castigated a waiting-woman or chastised a
slave for leaving it there. In fact I savor the multiple qualities of
that dust, each granule separate yet so finely ground that it
becomes one continuous coating; abrasive, yet silky smooth. I
could go on and on. For I believe God is in that grit. What else
in the world can be seen everywhere, in all things and in all
shapes? He's settling on the learning that's in those pages and
that is an endless source of comfort and reassurance to me. For
here in Alexandria they tell me that if I had not been the daughter of the great Duke Philip, ruler of Egypt by order of the
Roman emperor himself—judge and repository of knowledge—
no one would countenance my cleverness. That I am lucky to

be so educated and knowledgeable—they won't use the word "enlightened" for a woman; even books avoid that.

I was fifteen when Aquilinus, the son of the consul, proposed marriage. I remember that day. Father was elated, Mother was in raptures, even my brothers Avitus and Sergius wore a look of satisfaction that made it all the more difficult for me to refuse. But refuse I did. I have always done what I have had to do. It is something simple, something unerring—a union between the mind and the spirit, an acceptance that does not war with what-must-be.

"Why do you refuse?" pleaded Claudia, my mother. "What more do you want in a husband? He has power, status, prospects."

"But what are his qualities, Mother?" I asked. "What in particular commends him or sets him above other men?"

"Well, he is highborn," replied my mother. "That speaks for itself."

"It is not according to birth that I should choose my husband, Mother," I concluded, sad that I had to explain, dejected that I could not make her happy, "but according to morals and character."

My mother became worried. I heard her that night berating Father for allowing me the run of the library, for educating me so that I felt I was above the traditions of society and status.

A clever woman does not make a good wife, people believe. And what is a woman if she's not a good wife but a freak of nature? People call me beautiful and objectively I know what they mean. But this knowledge, this potential for argumentation and hypothesization and dissertation, this potential itself, rises between me and men like that diaphanous film between morn and dawn. The shape of one separated by an "n" at its end, the sound of the other by an "m" at its beginning.

Then there's the "d." M, n, d. "Mend."

Is that the message? The message you are sending me, God? For I believe that God is in that potential too, which I talked about earlier. Ever filmy, ever intangible, but how can you deny His enveloping, holding presence? It's like the womb of the mother I lost and found.

And it's the Christian God that comes closest to my experience of this silent, somber deity who overwhelms me though he refuses to take a shape or a form.

There are books in the library on every conceivable religion. The mighty Roman pantheon looks down on us from Olympus and, as my father recalls daily, favors our family. But they play games, those gods. And the father-god has a lively member that sometimes rules the forms he takes and the deeds he does. A god in the shape of a man, with the cardinal weaknesses of man. Of course, I concur, there is always a deeper and more profound lesson and significance in the most demeaning of his actions, but on the face of it I find his methods hard to support. I know there are wheels within wheels and flames within fire and the air that blows around us does so with an intent too subtle for us to know. Yet how can I avoid comparison when I know there was a man who even in earthly form, constrained by the same body and travails and relationships of mankind, lived a blameless life? His only fault lay in his decision to repudiate all family ties.

He was, of course, the man Jesus of Nazareth, a Jew. Scholars visiting my father's court tell us about this man. He has followers by the score, still turning to him, though he's been dead more than two centuries, crucified along with a common criminal, and they tell us desperately, compulsively, and in fear of their lives that he was the Son of God and there is but that one God who is the Father. The "disciples," as they are called, do not come to the court, we hear of them from the scholars— the historians and chroniclers and theologians and philosophers. People who observe and record the lot of mankind.

I have met these disciples. Their eyes bleed and their hearts plead and they beg us, not for their sake but our own, to clutch the hem of the garment of their Lord Jesus Christ. If we rest our brow an instant on his hem we are redeemed.

"Look at us!" they cry. "We are the living proof. We fear nothing anymore. We welcome death and persecution. It elevates us. We suffer it for the salvation of mankind."

Who are these people and made of what stuff to talk about taking on their shoulders the sins of humanity? It has never been done. It cannot be done.

Can it be done?

There are books written by men who knew this Jesus. I have some in the library, the teachings of a man called Paul. The disciples, like Paul, claim Jesus was the Messiah foretold by the Jews. The Jews say he is not. Their Messiah, they say, was to be king, not a lowly carpenter like Jesus. The disciples counter that he was King of Heaven and of the souls of men and he appeared in an ordinary walk of life so that he could be accessible to all men and so that all men could follow his path. It required neither money nor status, only a determined soul and a devout mind.

They haunt me, those bleeding eyes and pleading hearts, and something in me is repulsed by the sceptics who call this man a troublemaker and a charlatan with a unique talent for playing magic on the simple-minded masses. You see, I feel his formless God. I see Him in the desert granules of sand—and I know that it is only in such formlessness that infinity can lie and omnipresence, without which there can be no omniscience . . . and that is what they claim for Him, this One and Only God. In fact there is nothing that is good or terrible that they do not claim for Him. All-powerful, they call Him, all-seeing and all-knowing. Then in the same breath they call Him both all-merciful and the Great Judge, arbiter of harsh justice and the singeing of sins in a place called hell. And they *know* that what they say is true or they would not have the temerity to claim it. There is something of divinity in that. Seeing yet not seeing, believing yet not believing, being amorphous yet shaped like all things.

I knew I must investigate it.

"Come, Protheus and Jacincthus," I commanded my faithful slaves one day. "We must go and see these disciples in their own milieu."

The two men seemed willing enough and we set off, our minds and hearts open to what we might encounter. Protheus and Jacincthus had discovered that there was a large Christian enclave in a village not far from Alexandria and we headed there. Our first experience of the Spirit was the singing. Slow, gentle chanting that seemed to swell from the body of the earth and rise in a potent, massive wall all around us. My ears could not decipher a single word, yet my soul was moved, my hair stood on end, and I felt overwhelmed. As we got nearer we began to distinguish the words. They were simple. "All the gods are mere idols, the One God alone is God." I turned to Jacincthus and Protheus.

"I have studied all the categories of Aristo, the ideas of

Plato, the teachings of Socrates. But examine this sentence the Christians sing. It negates everything the poets, orators, and philosophers have ever uttered. The laws of society make me your superior; now I ask you from natural wisdom to accept me as your sister in Christ and we will follow his path together."

There were tears in the eyes of Protheus and Jacincthus as they nodded their heads. We embraced joyously and in a moment we had plunged into the singing, chanting embrace of the Christian crowd. From that day on life in the prefect's palace became a living hell. I knew I had to leave.

There are places called nunneries. I've investigated life in a nunnery—several in fact, and found they are not for me. There is no opportunity there to preserve and supplement knowledge. One abbess told me that my exceptional learning was what drew me to the temple. And of course she's right. But the second moment she insisted that I had acquired it so that I could give it away to God—a sacrifice. Not simply to present it to Him as a humble gift but to relinquish it, slit its throat, and leave it emitting ugly, lowly noises like the ram that Abraham slaughtered in the Jewish book. True, it was what I held dearest, but it was His gift—I could not throw it away to be replaced by mindless devotion and blind faith. Too many eyes were already open in all the parts of my being for me ever to be blind. Faith, I returned, was not always blind, devotion not necessarily mindless. Learning, I said, was God in me. She tut-tutted and shook her head and recommended humility and flagellation. And her eyes told me I was no longer a woman. Such arrogance! Such reasoning! The devil had surely entered me already. There was no place for me in her nunnery. And I did not regret it because I had no intention of entering it and living with her kind.

Sackcloth and ashes and whipping the devil.

I had never flinched from penance. I did it daily in one form or another. But how does one relinquish knowledge? I could not cut it away like those convert priests of Isis who struck off their penises and put out their eyes because their Lord Jesus Christ had said "If thy eye offend thee, pluck it out."

God have mercy, what a travesty! Harder by far to practice celibacy with penis intact, to look away from temptation when there's still sight to entice the eye.

But God, God, I know how You are, this Jew called Jesus describes the way I know You to be, it is His way that I must follow.

There's nothing else to do. I'm going to abandon my father, my home and yes, my beloved library, my asylum, my world, and my haven, to live a while in an abbey. Thoughts of continence, of having penises and not using them, have convinced me that I will be safe and secure in a celibate brotherhood. For I will learn and practice my knowledge and spend my time in the service and love of God alone.

Accordingly the next morning I left my father's palace. Protheus and Jacincthus went with me. We decided to seek admission in the abbey of St. Helenus. We had seen Helenus once when he was in disputation with a heretic. Helenus argued the word of Jesus patiently and wisely, but his erudition fell on deaf ears. Finally he looked up with eyes that seemed to shine with the veiled light of star clusters on a dusty desert night.

"I deplore spectacle," he stated, "but sometimes it is necessary." And Helenus instructed a group of people to light a fire large enough to hold a man. When it was ready, he addressed the heretic.

"I will walk through it first. If I come out unsmirched, it

will be through the grace of my God—and you must accept Him. If on the other hand, you come out whole, then I will accept yours."

When Helenus stepped into the inferno, the crowd gasped as one, a massive sigh of faith, so deep and united its coolness must have pacified the flames. We could see Helenus in the flare: its tongues licked and embraced, caressed and molded him. He seemed to revel and glory in the fire, performing a sort of ritual dance, almost as if cleansing himself of the impurities that clung to his form. Then a second gasp to welcome him when he stepped from it, a blaze still surrounding him as he stood free and looked the heretic in the eye.

"It is your turn now."

"Not I," retorted the heretic. "You will not catch me entering a fire. Only a madman would do that."

He looked wildly around for an escape route and, seeing none, hung his head. At a sign from Helenus the crowd parted and the man walked away, shamed.

"Pray God he will come back one day to be one of us. Meanwhile, may God ease the wounds of his shame."

Helenus's words impressed me even more than his dramatic deed. So it was quite natural that it was his abbey we chose for our retreat.

I cut off coils of long hair and my feminine appearance with it. I laid down my princely clothes, covered myself with the harsh, enduring fabric of my vocation that scrubbed off the superficial layers of my tender skin, replacing them in time with new, hard skin. It was calloused and coarse and altogether more suitable for my calling. But as we presented ourselves to Helenus's abbey, the chafing of my skin reminded me that I intended no deceit when I presented myself as a man. The brothers welcomed Protheus, Jacincthus, and me and accepted immediately my statement that I had left my past life and status behind me, and in order to avoid any future reference to it had decided to keep it secret. On the evening of our arrival at the abbey, Helenus called me into his chamber and fixed me with his twinkling glare.

"You are right to say you are a man," he said. "You do a manly thing."

My heart flipped in my chest and I opened my mouth to speak, though I never found out what I would have said. Helenus held a finger to his lips.

"We will pray," he whispered, *"Brother* Eugenius."

No reference was ever again made to my gender.

Life in the abbey was as close to perfection as I had dreamed. I learned so much about life and love and the fellowship of man. And though the emotion of worship is similar whoever the deity you worship, the fullness to bursting in our hearts, the release of the massive, explosive force of His presence in our tiny, worthless beings is impossible to explain. We found it streaming, streaming through our eyes, an ecstasy so profound and lasting, it drove away all thoughts of carnal desire from my fellow monks though we heard that there were monks who were not above the base pleasures of the flesh.

Daily we beat the lowliness and the shadow of the devil from our bodies. And once a month, when my clothes grew bloody, the brotherhood never questioned me. They assumed it was the blood of the wounds of flagellation.

The deception was the only blight on my happiness. I was satisfied in myself that God, who knew my body and my sex better than I did myself, looked favorably on my choice of lifestyle. Yet I was guilty of deception. I had not told my fellow monks that I was a woman. But it enveloped me, this new faith of mine, until every hair that grew from every pore of my skin strained to be immersed in it. Nothing existed for me other than the faith and the commitment to its propagation. I could not risk losing everything that held meaning for me. Not yet. I wasn't ready.

And how could I stay and fulfill my mission if I told them I was a woman? That old misogynist, the Roman Paul, also called Saul, had already debased women to an inferior grade.

Forgive me, Lord, forgive my trespasses, my frailty, my deception. O Lord, my God, Father of Jesus, give me a sign. A sign please, Lord, that You don't condemn me! Surely a small, disused portion of my vile body cannot invalidate my commitment, my devotion to You and Your Messiah, Jesus.

A sign, Lord, a sign.

I had my first sign when my womanly blood was withdrawn. Perhaps I was too jubilant at that moment, too eager and too quick to feel I was vindicated. But pride always goes before a fall. I chastised and humbled myself before God and wrenched the thanks from so deep a part of my soul that I became weak and could not get up.

The guilt of deception still lay heavy on my heart. Omission, commission—every time you are guilty of it, it is a new sin. So I begged daily for forgiveness. Then some years later, when I was older and more settled in the ways of the abbey, God sent the second sign. Helenus, on his deathbed, appointed me his successor.

I was created abbot.

It was, I knew, God's way of telling me that woman, man, whatever the shape of their genitals, if they did the deed and did it with purity of heart, chastity of mind, they were acceptable to Him. From that day on, I no longer feared rejection from Him after my death, though I still wondered, with terrible pain in my heart, what the brothers would feel if they knew they were led by a woman, for I loved them, each last one. Helenus had known, I comforted myself, and he had still chosen me. I remembered a night when we sat by the fire and he told us about his recent visit to Alexandria.

"The only daughter of the Roman prefect Philip is lost. They have searched everywhere for her. They have consulted diviners, they have sought advice from seers and sages. The wise men say that she has gone to beyond and become a star. Philip has constructed a statue of his daughter and ordered her worship."

As I crossed myself, I felt Helenus's gaze. It pierced my soul and saw that I was mortified. He was content. It may have been then that he decided.

It was not long after my appointment to the position of abbot that I was invited to Alexandria to attend a young matron from a rich and noble family. This woman, Melancia, had caught the quartan fever. I laid my hand on her hot brow and anointed it with oil of curative herbs in the name of Jesus, the greatest healer of all. Then I sat by her bedside, praying, until she opened her eyes. The fever had passed, I told her, and it was time to leave. But before I went, we would give thanks together. The woman thanked me, plied me with questions, begged me for words about the life and deeds of Jesus. I always found time to quench the thirst of a mind seeking this knowledge. I stayed and spoke to her. It was part of the precious burden of my calling.

I was surprised a few days later when this woman called for me again. Her maid said her fever had recurred. I sensed there was something amiss and asked her directly.

"I felt you would not come," she whispered, "if I said it was only to hear you speak about Our Lord. I planned this deceit and tricked you to come. Please let me confess and lighten my burden."

At first I thought I imagined Melancia rested her head on my knee a little too long when confessing, let her lips slide from my ring to my finger and even to my wrist when she sought my blessing. But then I realized she desired me. I was horrified but recognized it as a test. What could my Lord God be testing me for? The test, I decided, was sent for the woman, though a part of it may well have been a test of my own commitment, my compassion for a lost soul, my ability to spread out that divine net and save her from drowning.

I reminded her of my vow of celibacy. She threw herself in my arms and declared her passion. Her language was as explicit as a painting and full of a throbbing, knowing quality that I found repugnant. She spoke almost as if in a trance, describing how she saw my parts and which she wanted to touch, and how. Such delights she would show me, she promised, such pleasures, such rapture that heaven could not compete and that I would endure the flames of hell willingly as I sought more and more and more. A sort of paralysis came over me. This was the test. It had come at last. I saw Helenus in the flames and longed to be in them, to be purged.

"Help me, my Lord God!"

Was I to tell her that I could not love her because I was a woman? No. I had to speak to her as the abbot, to calm her, to convince her that the greater ecstasy lay in worship. The other would be too easy.

So I laid my hand on her head, like any holy man, with love and compassion and no thought of my own habit and what the loss of it would mean to me. At that moment I cared for nothing but the deliverance of her soul. Melancia, leaning her head a moment on my knee, began to breathe heavily, as if her body was preparing for sobs. I felt her hot, moist breath, the tears seep through my coat onto the skin of my thigh. Here it comes, here it comes . . . repentance, then the delightfully eased road of suffering to deliverance. Here it comes, here it is—but what!

The wretch's hands fumbled along my legs, my body, her lips like an animal's grabbing my clothes, dropping them! Oh, pain, the needles of her teeth sinking into my flesh, and oh, shame! I feel arousal—a strange responding of my skin to her ministrations. I feel forsaken parts of me turn liquid, my forgotten female parts suddenly tingle into life, Lord God! What is this? I swallow hard, clutching the edges of my seat. Temptation. This is temptation. My skin, my treacherously responsive skin, leaches my muscles of strength.

"Get thee behind me, Satan!" I howl as I stand. The chair falls over behind me, the woman in front of me. I shake and shudder as I look down at her, true daughter of Eve. And no wonder that men look down on our kind and revile us.

The diabola, she looks up at me, green eyes glinting, demon temptation focused upon me. I know you feel, her eyes say.

"I know you feel," she intones, fixing me with her green glare.

Strange that I never noticed before that greenness about her, my mind was so full of sand and the gold and sunshine of the desert and God in it.

It means nothing. For what is resistance without temptation but celibacy without a penis?

"Nothing," I say, and she laughs.

"Nothing?" she challenges, and lunges for my loins, thrusting her hand in my vibrating crotch. "I'll show you nothing." Her fist closes and there's nothing in it.

My time is up. I am exposed.

But no. She falls back, all of a heap.

"By Jupiter!" she gasps. "You're no man at all." (I turn into a statue.) "You are a statue. You have no feelings. Your member is as flaccid, as limp as your flappy clothing." Then, recovering herself, she snarls, "Or are you unmanned by lack of opportunity in all your years as a monk?" She places her hands on her waist and walks all around me, scorn dripping from her tongue, taunts like dagger-darts from her eyes. "Look at you and the pity of it. So beautiful, so young, so learned, yet you renounce the most blessed thing God sent."

I thought it best not to engage with her. Better to endure the mockery and the slurs on my brethren.

I was a Christian—a monk—above all. I should know that jeering and derision made wounds in which dwelt redemption. I made no defence and concentrated on holding back the arguments of intellect and learning that came so readily to my mind and that could in no time have reduced her jibes to nothing. I remembered the words of that nun all those years ago and dedicated my sacrifice in silence to my God.

"For You, Lord, I relinquish the power and protection that my knowledge gives me."

"I am a man of God," I said finally, "and I have sworn the oath of celibacy."

But Melancia would not accept that. She clutched her breasts and mouthed kisses—to tempt and ridicule me in a single gesture. But all I felt was anger.

"You deserve the name Melancia," I shouted, trying to restrain myself, "because you are full of blackness. A worthy daughter of the Prince of Darkness. You are a disgrace to your sex."

As I left I caught a reflective expression on her face. She would condemn me before I could denounce her. So it was no surprise to me when Philip, Duke of Egypt, Governor-General of Rome, had me seized and imprisoned to be fed to wild animals.

I lowered my head as I stood in his court, surrounded by spectators. How it hurt me to denounce another woman publicly! I would have carried Melancia's passion to my grave if only she had let me. But she had chosen a public revenge and here I was trampling on some part of the female essence in me that had bubbled and sung and survived and brought me a unique kind of joy even though I denied its physical expression. Womanhood, its way of seeing, knowing, giving, was on trial, and it was my duty to see it convicted.

Suddenly I saw a beam of light and thousands of dust particles dancing in it. An ecstatic movement—dance of life, dance of death—it was all the same. I knew I must trust my instinct. Womanhood has survived many onslaughts from the beginning of time. The malicious could use Melancia as a stick to beat women with. I was speaking out against abominable qualities—false accusation, perjury, lies. I did not forget to question whether my own manly demeanor was not also a kind of perjury. I knew that I would pay for it, then redemption would come. The cost was clear. In bringing down another woman, I would bring down myself. It had to be. The sand particles danced on. The outcome would be good.

"Tell us, you wicked creature," shouted Philip, "if it is your Christ who has told you to violate women of good family?"

"Our Christ has taught us chastity. He has promised eternal life to those whose souls and bodies are pure. As for this woman Melancia, I shall have no trouble establishing she is a perjurer. But it is better that I should suffer the outcome of my patience."

Then Philip summoned Melancia's servant-maid. She repeated her mistress's story. That I had visited Melancia on the pretext of seeing how she was and had attempted to defile her. I looked around me and was profoundly saddened to see what did not really surprise me: all those present believed the fabrications of Melancia and her maid rather than the words of a holy abbot. I knew my time had come.

I trembled with fear at the thought that the terrible wrath of God might fall on this woman. "Forgive her, Lord," I said, and the prayer was a whisper rather than a thought. For the Roman, my father, heard and demanded: "Forgive her? Forgive her what? It is you who stand before us accused of some very grave charges."

"My Lord Judge," I replied, my voice still shaking from the horror of discovering how evil can work a mind that once seemed open to purity, "I refute all the charges. I am celibate, have been so since the day I first entered the abbey. In fact, I have not known carnal relations in my entire life and have no intention of ever breaking my vow. And I know," I ended, overcome with the simplicity and truth of my conclusion, "that the Lord God is on my side and I shall accept His decision and understand that it is for my ultimate salvation."

There was a hush in the court and I looked briefly at Melancia. She looked pale, even gray, and the green in her eyes so vivid that it seemed to be disembodied and cast a green gleam over her face. The gray-green, the brackishness of her face, filled me with disgust followed quickly by pity. Had she come to me only because she wanted to seduce the young and beautiful abbot? Or had she lost her way while under my guidance? Forgive me, Lord! Forgive me in the name of our Lord Jesus Christ. Philip's words intruded on my thoughts.

"Why should I believe you, monk?"

Had my father always sounded so crude, so brutish? Or was it that I had forgotten how people behaved outside the abbey whose walls had protected me for so long?

"I am asking you to believe me, Philip," I replied boldly. "It is my word against Melancia's."

"Can you offer me proof?"

"Can Melancia offer you proof?"

"I've heard about you Christians," snarled Philip, who was once my father. "You bait us Romans and challenge us to torment you. You enjoy the torments and call them the route to salvation. Don't play with me, monk. I asked you if you can prove your innocence."

"I can, judge."

"Then stop wasting our time and do so."

"I will not," I insisted, "until I know what proof Melancia offers."

I heard the people cheer Philip. They preferred to believe him. Their laughter pierced me like arrows. I had to give up the struggle. The choice was simple: the notoriety could come to me or to my religion. It was time to give up my secret.

"Since you fail to recognize the lies of a highborn woman and her servant, since Melancia dares to accuse the servants of Christ of this crime, I shall unveil the truth. I want you to understand, it is not out of pride but for the glory of God."

I gripped the collar of my habit and pulled, ripping it to the belt.

"I am your daughter Eugenia."

Philip stared in disbelief and half stood, holding out his arms to me, when there was a mighty flash of fire. People ran this way and that, the guards entered and surrounded Philip, who immediately pulled me into his circle of protection, looking around to assess the danger and damage. I saw that miraculously no one had been hurt. Only the remains of Melancia and her maid stood intertwined in the aisles for a moment before their bones clattered to the side. God had done His will.

I pulled my robe together again, leaden in the knowledge that my time at the abbey had ended. I now had to find another way to continue my work. But then, God had been too kind to me already. The transition from one life to another had been too painless, too untroubled, and it was only now that I was to embark on my true journey.

I visited the abbey once more to beg forgiveness from my brethren for the long deception. Many of them saw my need. If I had admitted my sex, then I would have had no chance at all. And gender mattered less in a group of celibates than anywhere else. Of course I was a rare exception. Unique, in fact. And not an example many women should seek to follow. But of course I recognized I couldn't continue my work there. Before I left, I washed my robes for the last time, washed them lovingly before folding them away into the store. My hair had grown during my imprisonment, a ragged length in between man's and woman's. The long robes I wore were still those of a holy man, and that I would never change in this life.

I set forth on my mission to teach and spread the faith in Rome, stopping on the way in Alexandria. I found that Philip and Claudia had lost no time in converting to the faith, and my brothers Avitus and Sergius with them. Together, and a family once more (though what a different one, raggle-taggle and together), we started our long journey back to Rome to begin our work.

Thirty-odd years don't seem so long, as I emerge now from those sweet, desert memories. Time and the spaces in it seem to merge and blend. I cannot even remember how long it has been—ten years, fifteen—since Valerian ordered me bound to a rock and dropped in the Tiber. I remember the shrieks of terror from disciples, jeers and celebratory yells from Roman sceptics. I saw the skies turn as the rock made its onerous way to the watery depths of the river. And I prayed, prayed hard as the waters engulfed me. I felt the current carry me a little way, my arms float up weightless, the water making them dance. Release. I was free, free of my body, free from persecution. My soul had cut loose from the matter that had held it so long. But I was wrong. Free I was, but only from the rock. The ropes had loosened and recognizing the hand of God, I swam upward. Suddenly I felt myself lifted to the surface and a swirling firmness beneath my feet. I pressed my foot down: it gave, but no more than the sand in a desert dune. I knew there were layers upon layers, each holding up the other, that I could walk without fear of sinking. I walked and reached the bank to a cacophony of mixed slogans—some praising God, some branding me a sorcerer, some a charlatan.

Gallienus tested me too, in his reign. It became a sport for the Roman emperors—a game that they would win whatever the outcome for me, because one way showed a miracle, the other secured my death. I acquiesced. If I was to be a buffoon for the Romans for the glory of God, I was willing to play the part. This time the emperor put me in a burning furnace. How I missed Helenus then—but I came out alive, though choking and fevered. The flame went out before it ever touched my body. Nothing in my life changed.

I have been in this cell ten days now. The hunger that gnaws my belly is an old friend. It damages only the aging cell that imprisons the soul. But what is this? I see a light growing in the window of my cell. It's coming in and in it stands Jesus. Sweet Jesus. He holds out His hand and I put mine in His.

"Receive this food, Eugenia," he says, and I hear the exquisiteness of music in his voice. I am struck dumb, but my heart sings to his tune. He addresses the lost, cowering woman in me, he nourishes her with food for her body, food for her soul, glorifies her. Eugenia. It is Eugenia whom he touches and with whom he speaks.

"I am your savior and you have loved me with all your soul. I want you to know that on the next anniversary of my worldly birth I shall call you to my side."

Then the light and the music die and I am left thinking again of the dust, the sands I've sifted all my life to seek meaning, find sustenance, touch God.

I shall get up and walk out to find new pupils, give strength to old ones, spread the word among virgins. I know I have until Christmas. Until then nothing will change. The Romans will still resent my work and any day now I'll be put through another test. But my spirit does a dance of joy when I remember that my last incarceration is not far. Then I'll bow my head and let my soul rise above to watch it roll from my body, severed by a Roman sword. And my corpse will be immersed in dust.

Meanwhile, let them do their work—I have my own to finish! I am in no hurry, though I am ready now to present my proper body in its female glory to Our Lord Jesu Christ, *qui est benedictus in secula secularum.*

Amen.

A Tortuous Path

Princess Miao Shan, Goddess of Mercy, most Perfect Soul of the West, sat on her lotus throne in the clouds, watching with her inner eye as other clouds sailed by. Sometimes she saw her prior life drift past on those clouds. . . . It all seemed so long ago, so far away—worlds apart.

A smile bloomed in her heart. Nine years was nothing—not even the blinking of the Buddha's eye. Yet here she was, an immortal, and there, three thousand li and a decade away, was her father, still the same. He was not a bad man though he suffered the affliction of most kings: arrogance and an unshakable belief in himself.

"But aren't we all vulnerable sometimes to that feeling of greatness in ourselves?" she reminded herself, noticing a cloud hovering before her. Clouds brought her revelations, so she looked deeply into this one with all the concentration of her inner eye.

She saw King Miao Chueng, her father! How he writhed and tossed, twisted and threw himself around, like a twig on a fiercely raging sea. And he groaned, the king, like a birthing beast, howling its labor without anyone to help. Physicians came and went, small ones, big ones, true healers and charlatans, but no one had a cure for the king.

The princess's mind sought the cause; and there, concealed in the shadows of the room, discovered the God of Epidemics. When he found himself in Miao Shan's revelation, he explained the reason for his presence.

"The Master of Heaven sent me to punish this man who caused you suffering. So I have covered his body in ulcers. He has decreed that no one can help him but you."

When the vision passed, Miao Shan transformed herself into a mortal. She shaved her head and covered it with the hat of a physician-priest. She slung a gourd of pills on her hip and a bag filled with liniments over her shoulder and left Hsiang Shan to make her way to her father's kingdom.

"My father would not listen to me, but if he had I would still have been a princess, living a wordly life," she reflected, allowing her mind to travel back over the years that began her journey to Perfection.

The king was planning three weddings. First for his eldest born, then for the second, and finally he was ready for the youngest.

"Miao Shan," he said, "my favorite little wise thing. My third and most beloved daughter. You are to be married to the wisest, the handsomest, the finest man in the length and breadth of China. Would you prefer a first academician or a first military officer?''

"Father," replied Miao Shan, who was a solemn young woman, "I don't want to marry at all."

"Don't want to marry?" exclaimed the king. "How is that possible? I have no male heir and I have decided that your husband will be the one to succeed me. You must marry. That's what I planned. You are both to rule my country wisely and well when I am gone."

"But, Father, I don't want to be a ruler," insisted Miao Shan, grave now, because she knew that contradicting the king could mean death. "I decided when I was a little girl that I want to serve humankind while I live—and then, when I am dead, I can embark on the road to nirvana—the State of Peace and Perfection."

"Nonsense!" ruled the king. "You are my daughter. If I say you must marry, you must marry."

"Then I will marry," replied Miao Shan, thinking very fast. "But I beg you to find me a physician so that we can serve humankind together."

"A physician?" stormed the king. "You give and then take away in the same breath, Miao Shan. You defy your king, you play with your father's words. You deserve punishment."

So the king ordered the guards on duty to strip Miao Shan of her royal garments and leave her in the palace garden to wander alone and cold. Miao Shan welcomed the punishment. It was her first step on the road to Perfection. There with the winds and the rain, the sun and the moon as her companions, she prayed and worshiped and offered her thanks to the Buddha. This angered the king, who sent a message to the Foremost Lady of the Monastery of the White Bird.

"I am sending my daughter, the Princess Miao Shan," said the royal edict. *"Discourage her from being a nun and ensure she returns to my palace to be married to a man of my choice."*

Miao Shan was taken to the monastery. How happy she was that day! At last her father had accepted her needs and was helping her on the path to Perfection.

But what was this? The Foremost Lady was coming to the gates to greet her.

"Why are you treating me like a princess?" asked Miao Shan. "I have come here to work and be humble and attain Perfection. I would like to visit the temple and then I will be ready to begin work."

So the Foremost Lady sent Miao Shan to the temple. The incense was lit, the bells tinkled, the drums rolled, and Miao Shan prayed. Afterward the Foremost Lady told her how undesirable she would find life in the nunnery and advised her to return to her father in the palace. But Miao Shan was not discouraged and so the Foremost Lady put her to work in the kitchen.

"It was the beginning of my journey to Perfection," reflected Miao Shan. "Now, here I am in the form of a priest, on my way to visit my father again."

She swept together some dead leaves to make into a bed for the night. It was not much different from the bed at the nunnery, she remembered, laughing as the memory of her first encounter with the Immortals came back. How the Foremost Lady had tested her, how she had tried her. But Miao Shan had withstood it all. She had always known that the path to Perfection would be a tortuous one. Now she arranged her monk's weeds around her and lay down. The crackling of the dry leaves, the pricking of thorns and cankers, did not bother her. It only reminded her of the hardships of the world of phenomena and kept her steady in her devotion to the easing of its suffering.

By all standards she should have been unhappy during those early days in the nunnery. Yet she remembered the contentment she had felt as she washed dirty dishes, picked and prepared vegetables, swept the kitchen, trekked all the way to the nearest stream and back, each morning, each evening. Then came a wonderful moment. The Master of Heaven visited Miao Shan.

"I am touched by your vows," he declared, "and I have decided to lighten your burden."

Then he commanded the Spirit of North Star to activate the three agents of the world. The Gods of the Five Sacred Peaks, the Ministers of the Heavenly Dragon and Tu-ti, the Tiger Messenger. They were to oversee Miao Shan's life and help her where they could. The Sea-Dragon dug a well directly beneath the kitchen window, the Tiger fetched firewood, birds collected vegetables, and the Spirits of Heaven helped Miao Shan in her duties. Now she could devote herself to the pursuit of Perfection.

Well, when the nuns saw all this heavenly activity, they informed the Foremost Lady and she sent a message to Miao Shan's father to tell him that the princess was clearly chosen of heaven. And the next thing she knew was that five thousand of the king's soldiers had surrounded the nunnery and were setting fire to it.

Flames rose everywhere. Thick black smoke filled the rooms and choked and gagged the throats of the nuns who wailed and cried for mercy.

"It's your fault," they chided poor Miao Shan, "all your fault. If you had done as we said and returned to the palace, we would not be facing this disaster."

Miao Shan fell to her knees in the crashing debris of the nunnery. Nuns ran hither and thither for their lives, but she would not move. Hands folded, she prayed.

"Please save these good women and their nunnery."

When she had finished praying, Miao Shan drew a bamboo comb from her hair and pricked the roof of her mouth with its sharp teeth, drawing blood. Then she flung her head backward and spat the blood into the wind, upward, in the direction of the heavens. All at once rain clouds gathered.

It was as if the fire clouds of smoke had suddenly been transformed into rain clouds to quench the fire.

Miao Shan turned over in her woodland bed. The downpour that followed had put out every last flame and frightened off the soldiers.

"But it did not quell the king's rage," she recalled as the first light filtered through chinks in the rich tangle of branches above. It was time to rise and be on her way to her father's kingdom.

As Miao Shan rose, encumbered by the body of this priest, she remembered the last time she had been there.

Her father had brought her back in chains from the nunnery to his capital. He and his queen begged and cajoled her, gave her demonstrations of luxury and comfort, showed her their anger and despair. But Miao Shan spurned it all. Then Miao Chueng locked her up in a darkened shed for a night and a day.

"If you have not changed your mind by the morning," he threatened, "there will be no more chances for you."

The next morning, Miao Shan stood chained to the stake, ready for the sword.

"Today," she declared, "I am leaving this world for a nobler place."

But the spears of the lancers splintered as they touched her body; the sword broke in two as it approached her neck, and eventually the king ordered her to be strangled with a silken cord. Precisely as her soul left her body, Tu-ti leaped forward, placed a magic pill in her mouth, slung her over his back, roaring his tiger roar and waving his tiger tail and brought her to the forest where he laid her gently under a tree.

The next Miao Shan knew, she was floating in a strange, featureless world: no trees, no mountains, no running rivers. Where was she? What was she doing in this bleak, eternal space?

Then a youth appeared to her, blue as the sky, radiant as the sun.

"The Master of Heaven ordered Tu-ti to carry you away before your body could decay. He splintered the lances and broke the sword so that they could not damage your body. So when your soul returned triumphant from the lower regions, your body was reanimated. Now go to Hsiang Shan on Pu-to Island and there you will achieve Perfection."

· ·

And here she was, nine years later, a Perfect Being and back in the world to try and redeem her father. It was strange to regard the ways of the world as a human once again. People were not kind to priests. Oh, they asked for healing and passed on their scraps and obliged by providing them with water, shelter, and the occasional bowl of food, but underneath it all they thought of priests as scavengers, idlers who could not be bothered to work. Miao Shan laughed gently at the mirage of life and its miseries, knowing that there had been life before and there would be life hereafter for all these people, according to their deeds.

Had she not traveled the Ten Halls of Hell and watched the anguish of its condemned millions? Had she not seen the mutations and transformations they underwent before their souls transmigrated to another form? Was she not herself one of the fortunate who could choose to live free of a body unless, as now, she chose to have one? She had seen it all—and she had fallen to her knees in hell and prayed and transformed hell into paradise. And that was when the blue and radiant youth had removed her to Hsiang Shan because she could not be allowed to alter the decreed status. There had to be hell, there had to be heaven. That must not be changed.

Riding on her train of thought, Miao Shan arrived finally in her father's kingdom and found herself at the palace gates. Early one morning, the guards watched Miao Shan, a young priest, looking at the edict on the gates.

The king is indisposed. All physicians who read this royal proclamation are hereby commanded to attend the royal chamber immediately to offer a diagnosis.

*Any man who can offer the correct antidote will be well
rewarded.*

When the priest-physician had finished reading the de-
cree, she ripped it from the gate, crumpled it up, and cast it on
the ground. A brace of guards ran forward from each side.

"Hoi, priest! How dare you tear down the royal proclamation?"

"The proclamation is no longer necessary," replied Miao
Shan, "because I am going to heal the king."

"You?" jeered the guards. "You are going to cure the
king? You can't be more than twenty years old."

Miao Shan smiled. What could these men know about
her? She would forgive them for their rudeness: they didn't
know she had created this body for the single purpose of curing
the king.

She replied gently, "Tell the king I am here to end his
agony. Take me to him. I will find a cure."

"Shaven head, raggedy clothes, and he claims he has a
cure that even the first physicians cannot find," grumbled one
guard, but another felt in his body the calm power that came
from the priest-physician.

"I'll inform the king," he murmured, and disappeared
into the palace.

A few moments later Miao Shan stood before her father.
It was a curious sensation being his daughter yet not his daugh-
ter, a female soul in male garb. A deity disguised as a worshiper.
Once a victim, now a savior.

Quietly and quickly she examined the king and pronounced that she knew the antidote.

"But it will be impossible to find the ingredients," she informed the king.

"Then get out!" roared the king. "Is this a way of taunting me? To tell me that there is a cure but that I cannot have it?"

So Miao Shan left the palace and waited outside, praying. That night a spirit appeared to the king in a dream.

"This priest-physician is the only person who can cure you," said the spirit, and disappeared before the king had a moment to make any inquiries.

Immediately, he woke up the queen.

"Get that priest fellow back," he coaxed. "He is the only one who can cure me."

So the queen sent for Miao Shan.

"You need the hand and eye of a living person," she said.

"And how am I to get those?" bellowed the dismayed king. "What living person would give up a hand or an eye?"

The priest smiled; her face gave away nothing.

"There is someone who will sacrifice her hand and her eye to cure you. She lives in Hsiang Shan, three thousand li from this kingdom. Appoint two suitable men to visit her. She will not refuse them."

"Hsiang Shan?" pondered the king. "But doesn't it take a long period of abstinence to enter Hsiang Shan? And an even longer journey to reach it?"

Miao Shan nodded. "If they begin their preparations now," she promised, "I will see that their journey is swift."

So the king chose two ministers and after the appropriate penance and abstinence under the priest-physician's guidance, they were sent to Hsiang Shan, where they asked to see the woman whom she had talked about. As they were led to the altar where she could be found, Miao Shan transformed herself into a woman and waited to receive them.

The men bowed low before her and falteringly told her what they wanted.

"Of course," said the woman, handing them a knife. "Sever my left hand, gouge out my left eye, and return to your king with my gifts. The priest who sent you knows what to do with them. Your king will be healed soon enough."

The ministers hesitated. How could they bring themselves to sever the hand of a woman, to gouge out her eye? They were filled with repugnance.

But the woman's voice spoke inside their heads and calmed their hearts.

"You don't know the extent of this man's pain," the voice said. *"I do, and I am willing to make this sacrifice. Now, take what you came for."*

So one of the men gripped the knife in his hand, clenched his eyes against the chiding of his heart, and struck off the woman's wrist. Then, shaking, he handed the knife to his companion, who averted his head and gouged out the woman's left eye.

There was blood everywhere. It sprayed like fountains, tinting the atmosphere pink, sweetly scenting the crisp air. Attendants appeared with a tray of gold and placed the eye and the hand on it.

"Go at once to the priest-physician," commanded the woman, bleeding, bleeding. "He will know what to do."

The ministers fell to their knees to thank the woman, and returned to the king, where Miao Shan, once again in the guise of priest-physician, was waiting for them. She took their gory offerings and immediately set to work, creating an ointment which she applied to the king's ulcers. Barely had she finished smoothing on the ointment, when the king's ulcers disappeared from the left side of his body, leaving it clear and free of pain.

Well, the king was grateful, of course, but he could not understand why his right side was still afflicted.

"You will need the woman's other eye and her other hand to cure your right side," explained the priest. "Don't be concerned, she will be glad to give you what you need."

So the two ministers were once again dispatched to Hsiang Shan and presented themselves before the woman, who hardly seemed to have moved since their last visit. She sat behind the altar, her left eye streaming blood tears, the stump of her left hand dipped in a pool of dark, luminous blood.

"Here," she said, holding up her right hand and passing them the knife. "Do not be unhappy. I am glad to give you my other hand and eye. Take it."

This time the two men found the deed even harder to do, but the woman urged them on with comforting words until they had sliced off her right hand and gouged out her right eye. They bowed deeply before the bleeding woman. When they arose, they saw in amazement that the blood had stopped flowing. Then her eyes and her hands were restored and finally, whole again, she faded into the air.

"How like Princess Miao Shan," they thought, but neither spoke the thought aloud.

Once again, when they returned, Miao Shan, transformed from the woman into the priest, was waiting for them. Once more she ground the hand and eye into an ointment and this time applied it to the right side of the king. Immediately, his ulcers disappeared.

The king was grateful beyond expression. He offered the

priest-physician wealth and titles and lands and begged him to stay on in his kingdom as Priest of Priests and Physician of Physicians, but the priest would only bow his head and decline.

"Your world has nothing that I want. I must return where I belong."

"Only one other person has ever refused me like this before," thought the king. "She too rejected everything I could offer."

For the first time, the king regretted what he had done to his daughter and wept unreservedly. The priest watched silently, then, saying a farewell prayer, turned to go. A cloud drifted down and as the king and his courtiers watched in amazement, she climbed on and floated away.

A moment later a note fluttered down from the skies.

I am one of the Teachers of the West. I came to cure you and so bring glory to the True Doctrine.

The king turned to his two ministers.

"The woman who made the sacrifice, how did she look?"

"Like Princess Miao Shan, Your Majesty," they said.

And that was how it happened that King Miao Chueng handed over the throne to his two ministers and embarked on the path to Perfection.

A Gown
of Moonthreads

*S*ob. Sob, sob, sob.

The princess pulls the feather-filled land of multicolored cartouches and finely embroidered palm motifs over her ears and turns over. What is disturbing her sleep?

Snuffle, snuffle.

Is it an insect? She buries herself deeper beneath the quilt. Go away. Let me sleep. The moon had looked cold and metal-bright in her skies tonight, when the princess gazed out before gliding into her bed. Frosted over. On nights like this the moon felt chilly and deepened her glow in an attempt to get warmer. It was on a night like this, according to a Jewish tale, that the moon once went to the sun and demanded a gown to keep her warm. And it was on nights like this when she was shiny-cold that Lamia, the demon temptress, came out to shower in the light and reveal herself in all her glorious beauty. Then she did her sinister dance and lured innocent men into her house of golden illusions and in time gave birth to the child of each encounter. But, the princess had reminded herself, the Lamia lived in neighboring Libya, though some said she traveled to other countries too. Followed the moon.

The princess snuggles into herself, safe, her nose savoring the fragrance of incense trailed on the silk like a lingering memory. It whispers to her and she drifts. She hovers in the land between sleep and non-sleep, enjoying the sensation of letting go.

Sniff. Sniff. Sniff. She sits up with a terrible shock. Her hair is a dark rain cloud around her golden disc of a face. Her eyes flash and nearly, nearly, there is a roar of thunder about her too, for sleep has not let go of her voice and it is deep and rumbling.

The thunder settles, the lightning dims, eyes full of sleep draw down their lids. She falls back on a great silken bank of cushions. On the patchwork, moonthreads embroider more moons to embellish her sleep, silver and gold. Warmly, they cover her. Palms grow silently back into their shape. She drifts into dreams about the story of the moon told by the Jews. After the moon had demanded the gown, a humble young tailor offered to travel strange, magical lands in search of a fabric that would stretch and shrink to fit her on nights when she was cold. Nights like this one. When he found it the moon would be warm.

Sob. Sob. *Sob*. The princess throws herself from the side of her bed, sleep gone.

"I can't bear it. What is going on. What is it? An insect? No, too loud. An animal?"

Snuffle, sniff, sob-sob, sob.

She creeps over to the window. Should she wake the maids sleeping next door? They do not seem at all disturbed by the noise.

Sob.

"Who are you?" she calls, moving to the window. "If you are a demon, be gone. If you are human, show yourself to me."

In the light cast down from her window, a lithe figure appears. How silvery he looks, how gossamer, how beautiful. Is it really the light from my window? she wonders. Or is it the moon mingling with the flame-light to do magical things? The story about mooncloth drifts back into her mind. It is a story about achieving the impossible. But then, she reflects, does the meaning of "impossible" exist for us women? We create from our bodies, and those creations give us immortality. What can be more impossible than to die and live at the same time? She wonders if this man is wearing a garment of moonbeams.

How strange it is that a million thoughts can pass perfectly crystallized in the words of the mind—yet when you speak them, they take an age. It is a special language of the mind unfettered by words, free to enmesh all possibilities.

"Who are you?"

"A man, not a demon."

"I know that," she replies dreamily. "I know that you're not a demon." But, she thinks to herself, you could be a fairy creature. How beautiful you are. Standing there bathed in a shower of moonshine, you could be a son of Lamia. Aloud, she speaks harsher words.

"Why are you making such a noise outside my sleeping chamber?"

"I didn't know anyone slept here."

"But why are you crying? And what are you doing here so late at night? How did you get into the palace anyway?"

He throws his arms across his eyes and she flinches. He is fending her off, this delicate moon creature. She must be gentle with him, or he might disappear. Into the gauzy light of the frosted moon.

"I came here to die." His voice falls like dull, heavy thuds on a gong that should throb and clang the sounds of celebration.

"Die." Her eyes are circles, her mouth trembles. "Die? But you are so young and beautiful. Why do you want to die?"

"Because," the moon creature replies with determination, "my life is over. I have nothing to live for."

She makes up her mind swiftly. She cannot let him die.

"Come up," she commands, her tone imperious. "Then you can tell me all about this matter. You are talking in riddles and I find riddles very hard to solve. Specially"—and here she giggles—"when I've been woken up from a very frothy sort of a sleep."

She thinks of the impossible—moonbeams and fabrics woven from them—as she waits for him to make his way up. Her finger traces the line of her throat a moment, feathers on satin. Can he shape-shift, she wonders, from man to demon? If he looks from near as he did in the moon lake outside her window, she will persuade him to spend the night in her bed, all entwined in limbs and covered in palm fronds and feathers.

She sees magical visions as she slides the heavy bolts of her doors into place. She wants no interruptions while this fairy man is here.

And suddenly here he stands. She inhales sharply. She has never experienced anyone, like this, with her body, before. Without even a touch. It is as if he is melting into her, limb to limb, body to body even from a distance of about two yards. She pulls herself together and asks him to sit down. She pours him an aromatic drink from her salver of blown glass encrusted with silver. It has come all the way from Egypt. The men there have found a way of dyeing glass and its colors glitter like jewels, sometimes blue and sometimes green and pink. They call it lusterware. It fills her eye and pleases her.

"Araq," she says as she stands over him, making sure he drinks. She savors the deep consonants that issue from her throat.

He is hungry and drinks eagerly. She puts a plate of sweetmeats and savory treats in front of him. She nourishes him with food and care. She can feel him becoming stronger. She feels like mother and mate in one. The quintessential female, made to contain men in so many different ways.

"Now, tell me," she says, settling down next to him when he has finished. "Tell me your story from the beginning."

His father died two years ago, he explains. He was a rich merchant, so rich and so successful that he had hoped his wealth would serve many generations. He was highly thought of in Casablanca, where they lived, and just before dying he called this young man, his only son, to him.

"Jakob," he said, "what will you do with all the wealth that will soon be yours?"

"Why, Father," replied Jakob, "I will make merry, I will feed people and be fed by them. In short, I will make up for your austerity and enjoy life as a man of your wealth should."

"Alas! For shame!" said the old man, his death a little

closer as his heart sank with the words of the boy. "Then all my work has been a waste."

That was the death of him. And Jakob, unaware of his own part in his father's demise, proceeded to keep his promise. In a year, the wealth was gone. All gone—not a penny, nor an asset, nor an unrecovered debt. So Jakob went to his father's friends.

"I'm going to set up in business," he vowed. "I'm going to work really hard and make it up to my mother for subjecting her to this double disgrace of poverty and a prodigal son. I'm going to succeed."

But no: every time he saw the glint of gold, the flash of silver, he was away into wonderland, and business and industry were forgotten hellholes. Eventually he was deeply in debt and had to leave Casablanca. Abandoning his impoverished, disgraced mother to fend off his debtors with the force of her own dignity, he arrived here in Marrakesh, determined to make amends. Immediately he called on his mother's brother. Old Noah lent him money, then more, then a final sum. And he saw that the boy was doing no good with it and it was doing the boy no good. Threats and warnings of a debtor's lot had not so far been much use, so he thought he would secure his money with a threat so dire that the boy would be turned into a man.

"If you can't return the money to me with interest by the end of the year, you will pay for it with a pound of your own flesh. And I'll cut it from your body forthwith."

"I agreed," weeps Jakob, looking into the eyes of the princess. "And I intended to keep my promise, but the habit of luxury is hard to break—two years of it is like a lifetime of any other addiction."

He hangs his head. "I can hide no more and I can weep no

more. I have to appear in a court of law to give an account of myself, and there my uncle, old Noah, will take my flesh. He says that since I have brought my mother into penury and he will have to support her from now on, I should be punished in some way."

He beats his breast and his head and she leans forward and stays his hand.

"I came here today hoping to get killed—you know, a stranger found wandering in the quarters of the king and his family." And here he begins clamoring and weeping again. "But even death has spurned me. Do you see my accursed destiny—no guards at the gate. I wandered in, thinking it would be a matter of time before they found me. But no—not one of them has seen me, and that's why I'm here in your chamber, with you."

He sobs and laments so much that she wonders if she should be offended.

"It's not so bad, is it?" she murmurs, wondering if there is a lost sweetheart somewhere in all this. "Here with me, is it so bad?"

Boldly she asks, and he stares at her with glazed eyes.

"Lovers there were scores," he says; "sweethearts none."

Relieved, she reaches out and touches his face, wiping away the tears with the finest of muslin soaked in cooled essence of rose.

"Stay with me tonight," she breathes, "and tomorrow I will make sure your problem is solved."

"No, no!" he gasps. "I don't want any money. Even if you pay off my debt, what then? Even if you give me a fortune after that, what then? If I could fritter away, twice over, a fortune as big as my father's, I can do the same again with a third."

"I am not offering you money," smiled the princess. "Only a solution."

She leads him to her bed and she undresses him and settles him down. Naked they are startlingly similar in height and skin and suppleness. Their bodies mold and mix well. He knows about featherbeds and silk on skin and pleasing women.

"But," she thinks afterward with satisfaction, "this clinging and holding and sleeping with his head on my breast, this is for me alone. I am his savior."

She loves his helplessness and remembers his reliance and trust long after he has gone. She misses his soulful look, his whispered demands for reassurance, his appeals to be held and looked after. She has never met a man like him before. She is determined to solve his problem and win his hand.

"I have the same problem," she realizes, "as the young tailor in the Jewish tale, the one who was looking for the cloth made of light. And I must keep searching for the impossible until it becomes real."

So she spends many hours racking her brain. She pores over the documents Jakob has left her, she bends her mind around the problem in this way and that, she scrutinizes books on the law. Eventually, she comes up with a plan. She is nearing her goal, just like the point in the story when the tailor wandering in strange lands found the country where the queen wore a robe woven from mooncloth. The princess puts the idea to her father's lawyers. No, they laugh, why does the princess waste her time on matters of law? They are not for her pretty head. The law is a mighty beast, it will not be driven by a woman's notions.

"But," she reminds herself, thinking of the story, which has now become a sort of parable, "even though the courtiers told the tailor the queen was too unhappy to tell him how to weave mooncloth, he went ahead and asked her anyway."

The tailor spoke to the queen, who told him that the fabric of her dress was unraveling. The secret of how to weave mooncloth, she told him, had long been lost. Would the young man be able to weave some more so that she could go to her daughter's wedding? The tailor agreed to try. He knew he had the will.

The princess too decides to disregard the courtiers and puts her thoughts to her father, the king.

"Isn't my daughter wily?" he guffaws. "She wants to trick the law with witty words."

"Then will you let me carry out my plan?" asks the princess eagerly.

The king shakes his head.

"In this court you hold sway—" He thumps his heart. "In this court you will always be heard—" He motions around the royal court. "But in that court where laws are formed and feuds are resolved and life and death hang in the balance—I cannot let you interfere. The men who deal with such matters are wise and good and just and cannot be instructed by a woman. Even if that woman is my beloved daughter."

The men agree that the princess is bored. The king commands her companions to find better ways of amusing her. He consults his ministers about involving her in matters of state.

"There is a woman in Sind, all the way across the great ocean," he says, "a princess of a place called Bhambore. And the king her father has put her in charge of tourism and art. It is not unthinkable to entrust a noblewoman with affairs of state, so long as they are light and will not try her too hard."

But the princess was determined. If an ordinary tailor

could find a robe fit for the moon, she could certainly solve Jakob's problem. And she continued to try and find a man of law willing to put her solution into practice and win the case for Jakob.

The princess knew her idea was a good one, but all the lawyers responded in the same way. The thought was too clever by half to be entertained in a court of law.

Well, there was nothing else to do. The princess, too, had the will. She had made a promise to Jakob, and by God she was going to fulfill it. And when it was done, she would ask him for his hand, having won it fair and square. The young man in the story, she recalled, just sat down by a window and concentrated hard on finding a way. Night and day became one for him in those hours, and as he pored over the cloth and its weave and held it up to the moonlight to see better, the moon turned liquid and poured down her light along moonbeams to blend with the fabric. And the fabric grew and grew and grew until the gown was replenished and repaired. A simple solution. But you had to find it to realize its potential. So the princess pored over the warp and woof of the garment Jakob had woven for himself, held it to the light of her mind, and tried to scrutinize it as carefully as possible. The moon would turn liquid. It would flow down to her.

Soon enough, the day came. Jakob arrived in the court of law—his hair disheveled, his beard grown—jumpy as a hunted thing. She watched from her veiled position and saw that though his general demeanor was despairing, his eyes still carried the calm and the trust she had put there and her heart swelled and overflowed. Like the light of the moon. And she hoped the moonthread would work its miracle for her as it had for the young tailor.

· ·

The witnesses are brought on, one after another, after another, all testifying to Jakob's profligate ways.

Now the judges fix Jakob with penetrating looks and ask him what he has to say in his defence. Jakob hangs his head.

"It is true, it is all true."

"But what were you thinking when you signed this document?" asks his lawyer.

Jakob sees him for the first time and there is fear on his face. He is so young, this lawyer, the skin on his face still smooth and pink. The fabric of his dark legal cloak is crisp and new, it whispers as he moves. And it is of strange, voluptuous cloth, enigmatic as the night. Deep and satiny and enveloping.

"But," Jakob tells himself, "the princess promised and she would not choose carelessly."

He decides to give this young man his all.

"I was thinking," he mumbles, "that the risk involved would force me to change my ways. But I failed again."

The spring chicken of a lawyer looks brashly at the judges.

"This proves his goodwill, does it not, honorable sirs?" His manner is arrogant and confident and Jakob shudders at the consequences it might bring. "For who, in your vast experience, have you known to pledge his flesh against his word? No one, I feel sure."

The old men, bearded and beady-eyed, confer, their voices like the buzzing of bees.

"We are sure of his good intent. Nevertheless, he signed a contract. Now he must honor it. Good intentions, after all, are the foundation stones of the road to hell."

The lawyer's head drops, acquiescent.

"I agree with your wisdom. But this young man, Jakob, stands to lose his life if he honors his pledge. I must therefore ask that the venerable gentleman, his creditor, ensures that the exact amount of flesh is cut from his body. Not a shred too much—for it is not like a bag of coins that can be replaced. Nor an ounce short, because this young man is determined to keep his word. Jakob has not promised his life—nor indeed has his creditor demanded it."

With a flourish the lawyer finishes speaking and withdraws to a corner, leaving the court hushed, awed, dumbfounded.

Jakob's head lolls. All is surely lost. This playing with words, this attempting to put one over on their lordships, this will never do.

But what is this? Once again the judges are buzzing like bees. They sit up and look with admiration at the lawyer. They summon him forward with the creditor.

"The law," they say, "is nothing if not about the precise sense of words. And this young man is a welcome addition to our ranks. It is his job to prevent undue damage to his client. Can you, Noah, guarantee to take the precise amount of this young man's flesh?"

"I can take it cautiously," offers the creditor, "then weigh it and if it is short, add a little more."

One of the judges shakes his head. "That would be too cruel. We cannot subject him to the knife twice."

The creditor preens himself.

"Then I will be content with less," he says, affecting a posture of magnanimity.

"Oh, no!" protests the lawyer. "Is it fair, my lords, to subject my client to this barbarous punishment yet leave him still burdened with the guilt of an unpaid debt and open to criticism for reneging on an agreement? Every part of his pledge must be fulfilled. He must be absolutely free of it.''

The judges nod agreement. They buzz again, their heads and beards forming a bizarre circle.

''The fine must be exact,'' they pronounce. ''A pledge is a pledge. It must be paid in exact terms.''

''Well then,'' puffs the creditor, ''I am being forced to forgo my right to the penalty. I will accept my money.''

''Never!'' remonstrates the lawyer. ''Money was offered to you three days ago. You refused. Another settlement was offered two days ago, and finally this morning on the doorstep to the court. You refused three times in all.''

The judges clap in unison.

''Do you forfeit this debt and forgo your right to take a pound of this man's flesh?'' they ask. ''Readily and after consideration? You must understand you are under no constraint to do so.''

The creditor, red and breathless, pants his assent. The judges sweep out, praising the lawyer. Today's defense will become famous all over the world in time, they rejoice. People will write about it. Their laughter can be heard from next door as Jakob rushes over and thanks the lawyer, begging him to convey his thanks to the princess.

Then Jakob returns to his squalid quarters.

''If only,'' he says aloud, ''if only I could see her just once again.''

''Granted,'' her voice rings out from his door. The princess has come to see him. Here. In his ugly, odious lodgings.

''Your precious feet,'' he mumbles, ''they will be tainted by my floor.''

"I know," she breathes. "That is why I have come to take you away from it all, to a floor that will not taint them."

He falls to his knees and she strokes his hair.

"I'm so grateful to your lawyer, to you . . ."

"Let's leave this place," she urges, her senses assaulted by the ugly surroundings. "It smells terrible."

He rises as she tugs a lock of his hair and buries his face in her neck.

"Did the lawyer tell you all that happened in court to-day?"

"I was there," she replies, "I was part of it all. Now, come with me, my carriage is waiting to take you away."

In the coach, as they embrace and kiss, she reaches behind and plucks out a bundle of dark, slithery new fabric.

"I wore this in court today," she says. "It is my gown of moonthreads."

WHAT WILL BE
WILL BE

There was a country and it had a king, though for you and me, God is king, for He is one, but kings there are plenty. My story has four but I begin with the first of these, the one that launches the actions of my story, for that is generally where the storyteller begins to tell.

One day this king went out hunting as is the way of kings when suddenly he felt a shadow fall over him. The fearsome fingers of premonition clenched themselves around his heart, squeezing the breath from him, making him gasp, while at the same time a wizened, shadowy hand wrenched at the bridle of his horse and pulled it to such a screeching, whinnying halt that a lesser horseman would have lost his seat. As the horse stopped, the king's eye fell on the owner of the hand—the most horrible-faced hag he had ever seen. She was tall—her head came level with the back of his Arab. Her hair formed a massive halo around her head, it was so matted and tangled. Rushes and twigs dangled from it and in places it moved as if live creatures lived there. I don't mean lice and fleas and small things whose natural habitat that is, but bigger ones, birds maybe, even rats and, who knows, perhaps a coiled snake or two. Her face the king could not see, though he peered and squinted. It seemed shrouded in shadow and her two eyes shining orange from it like two fiery round embers, hot and dangerous. She wore next to nothing on her lithe, strong body and when she spoke, her voice was a hiss.

"I am What-will-be-will-be," she spat at the king, "and you will taste my power."

"What do you want?" the king asked, his eyes reacting to every twitch of her talonlike fingers. "If I can grant it, it's yours."

The hag cackled and the bristles of the king and his horse stood on end with the terror that lurked and swilled inside them.

"*You* grant me what I want?" she screeched. "*I'm* the one who's doing the granting here. And what I'm asking you is this. What will be will be—no one can change that. And you have some years of ill fortune due to you. Do you want them now, king, or would you rather have them later?"

The king hesitated. It was a difficult question and how could he answer it without asking his queen? After all, her life would be affected and so would that of their two young sons and the two sisters, their wives. Though, of course, the young princesses would go where their husbands went and do as they were told.

"May I tell you tomorrow, Mother What-will-be-will-be?" the king asked. "I cannot answer your question without talking to my queen."

To the king's surprise, the witch agreed immediately.

"Tomorrow," she hissed, "in this place. Kismet is kismet: now or tomorrow, it will fulfill itself. Meanwhile, fare you well."

Relieved and grateful, the king thanked the witch and made his way home, where he immediately went to the queen and told her what had happened.

The queen thought for a while.

"We are both quite young," she said sadly. "Perhaps it will be easier to get over our misfortune now so that we know we'll be comfortable in our old age. Tell the old witch that we would prefer to face the harsh part of our kismet now. Then we can look forward to happiness in our old age."

The king agreed. After all, if they chose to save their ill fortune for later, the intervening years would be blighted with the anxiety of waiting for it to strike. So the next day he mounted his horse and set off to meet his destiny who, sure enough, was waiting for him as she had promised.

"What have you decided, then, king?" she hissed, her face still in eclipse, the murkiness of calamity enshrouding her in a dark and terrifying shadow of mystery. And what can be more frightening than the Unknown—and that too, an Unknown known to be harsh and cruel and unrelenting?

Well, the king, whatever his weaknesses, was still a king and still the proprietor of his crown, so his courage intact and his resolve firm, he said without dismounting from his horse, "My queen and I have decided that we will face our ill fortune now, while we are still young and strong, then we can recoup our fortune and die in comfort and dignity."

The hag raised her gnarled finger to the skies.

"So be it," she pronounced. And the king left, his heart full of fear. When he returned home, he found that a neighboring king had amassed his army on the borders of our king's country and there was nothing to do but to fight back with all he had. They fought hard and they fought bravely, but kismet will have her way and we already know the outcome. That the king lost in spite of his best efforts and he and his family had to flee with nothing but the clothes on their backs.

For four days they ran, hiding here in a cave, cowering there under a dung heap, scrounging for food like the stray cats and dogs that littered the streets of their kingdom—or the kingdom that was once theirs. Hunger is a terrible thing. On the fifth day they barely cared anymore for their lives—it was their bellies they needed to fill. Berries and fruits may be good enough for ascetics and hermits used to living in the forest, but the cruel winter was harsh on this family, used to the warmth of a full belly, a roaring fire, and the enveloping embrace of a wool blanket.

Then the king spoke to his wife, and his sons. And though his words were the words of one fallen a long way from the virtue of a king, he expected and extracted from them the obedience due a ruling monarch.

"Tonight when the two princesses are asleep, we will leave them here and move on. That way, we at least will be able to keep body and soul together with what we can get. They are just two more mouths to feed."

The princes, their husbands, protested, but their mother motioned to them to be quiet. The king had lost enough in the past few days and disobedience would humiliate him beyond endurance. So with heavy hearts, the boys obeyed their father and that night, while the two princesses lay sleeping, innocent flowers, the others ran off and left them.

Well, when the two sisters awoke in the morning they found their family gone.

"We must find them," declared the older sister immediately.

"But they have left us here to fend for ourselves."

"Ah," replied the older one dismissively, "we would have done the same in a few days. Besides, we can do better because without them no one will recognize us."

"But where will we find them?" asked the younger, feeling hurt and frightened.

"Leave it to me," responded the older. Relieved that she did not have to take the initiative, the younger followed obediently.

Together they set off to the nearest town, where the older sister (we will call her Wahda) sold a ring she had and from the proceeds bought her sister (Sughra, the younger) a set of clothes of the kind that would not distinguish her as a princess. Herself she dressed as a man, because cities are full of people of both good character and bad and two beautiful, inexperienced women on their own would not have been safe there. Then they made their way to the capital of the kingdom. There in the marketplace, Wahda made inquiries until she found a modest house which she bought and where the two sisters began to live.

Each morning Princess Wahda would dress herself in

men's clothes and visit the court of the king and keep a close watch on all the scores of people who were in and out of there. She spoke to the regulars and she chatted to the visitors and generally did all she could to find out if anyone could give her any information about her family. And every day, the king saw this delicate and noble-looking young man come into his court, greet him with the utmost courtesy and the air of one who knew about courts and kings, then proceed to mix with all and sundry in a most gracious manner.

He became more and more curious.

"Go and ask that young man who he is," he commanded one of his courtiers. "And tell him the king has commanded him to come and pay court."

As soon as she received the message, Wahda presented herself to the king, bowed deeply, and said how honored she was to be noticed by the king and to be in his presence.

"But why did you never present yourself before?" demanded the king.

"Why, Your Majesty, it never occurred to me to be so bold," she replied.

"Well," said the king, "do you plan to stay in my kingdom long?"

"If it is acceptable to you, Your Majesty, yes, I do."

Then the king asked the princess her circumstances and she explained briefly that she came from a noble family who had suffered misfortune and that she was now the protector of her only sister and had somehow to make a living for both of them.

"Well," said the king, delighted, because he had taken a fancy to this young man (or woman—it's all the same at the moment, because he thinks her a man, though we know she's not). "Will you work as my bodyguard?"

The princess did not hesitate. "I would be honored, my lord."

The king was delighted. "Done! From this day on you are my personal bodyguard."

Well, the king gave his new bodyguard a mansion befitting a personal aide of the king, and the two sisters moved into it and began living a life of luxury. As for the king, he barely let his bodyguard out of his sight.

Now, one night when Wahda was on night duty and the king was sleeping comfortably after a hard day's work, she heard a most hideous howl. Quick as a flash, she checked the casements, then rushed to the door. No one. Not a soul.

Then suddenly, once again, the most terrible wail.

The bodyguard locked and bolted the king's chamber so that no one could enter, then went quickly down the steps and outside, following the shriek, which repeated itself at regular intervals. After a while she found she had come to the edge of a burial ground on the outskirts of the city. Looking around her, she saw a row of gallows with dead men suspended from several of them. But surely, she thought, shuddering, it was not possible that anyone here could be responsible for those fearsome noises. It was unthinkable, surely, that one of these criminals intended to be hanged to death could still be alive? The thought was too macabre and the bodyguard was about to leave the place, when once again the mournful moan assailed her ears and she turned around to see the silhouette of a woman, her arms raised above her head as she tried to reach for the legs of a man dangling from the gallows.

The bodyguard hurried to her.

"What do you want, Mother?" she asked. "Your cries are so loud, they can be heard in the king's bedchamber."

"As well they might," lamented the woman, all slumped and lifeless now. "That is my son there. My precious child, hanged by order of your king's judges for a crime he did not commit. And he's hanged so high that I, unfortunate wretch, curse my feeble bones, cannot even reach his face to kiss."

And she let out another ear-shattering howl.

Wahda clapped her hands over her ears.

"I understand your sorrow," she reprimanded, "but your howls will not bring your son back to life."

"I know," conceded the woman, wiping away her tears. "But do me a kindness, son. Lift me up on your shoulders so that I can kiss my son's face a last time. Then, I promise, I'll go away quietly and never come back."

Relieved, Wahda lowered herself, allowed the woman to climb onto her shoulders, and raised her up to kiss the hanged man. The woman leaned her face to the hanged man's, then with sudden vitality and life she sank her teeth into his neck and began sucking his blood, slurping noisily as jets of warm, sticky blood flew here, there, and everywhere.

Wahda realized at once that the creature on her shoulders was a vampire ogress, not a bereaved mother. In a flash, still trembling with the horror of what she had seen, she threw the creature to the ground and flew at her with her sword. Though she could not fly, the ogress had the swiftness of magic and was on her feet and away like a streak. But something lay glittering and gleaming on the floor in the most glorious patterns. It was a piece of the ogress's garment that had been concealed beneath her dark cloak.

Wahda retrieved the cloth and hurried back to the king's chamber.

The king meanwhile was waiting in an absolute fury. One of the howls had awakened him and he had called for the bodyguard who he found had gone. Worse still, he needed to relieve himself and since no one but the bodyguard had the key, he was well and truly stuck. Locked into the chamber, he became increasingly uncomfortable. It made him feel defenseless and he was not pleased.

"And where were you when you were supposed to be guarding my life?" he thundered.

"I went in search of that howl," replied the bodyguard hastily, and told him the story.

The king, still sulky from his humiliating experience, demanded proof.

"This fabric," said the bodyguard, unfolding the fabulous piece of cloth. Oh, how it shimmered and shone, but neither the king nor the bodyguard could make out whether it was velvet or satin or brocade. It was soft and diaphanous and embroidered in such lush and exotic patterns that neither one of them could claim to have seen anything so wonderful before.

"I'll give it to the queen," decided the king. "She may have use for it."

Well, when the queen saw it she so fell in love with it that she wanted to have enough for a whole suit of clothes.

"Get me more," she demanded, "or I shall never be happy again."

"Get me more," repeated the king to his bodyguard, "or I fear I shall never have peace again."

"But how, sire?" pleaded the bodyguard. "I got the cloth from a vampire. I didn't even see where she went—it was like a streak of light—a falling star. Who knows where it falls or if it falls at all?''

"Oh, this is just pretty talk," grumbled the king. "I must have that cloth for the queen or life won't be worth living."

The bodyguard reasoned and pleaded and appealed to the king's better judgment, but he would not relent.

"You will be handsomely rewarded if you bring back the cloth," he insisted. "And pay with your head if you don't."

So the very next day Wahda set off in search of the precious cloth so that the queen could have her suit of clothes.

"If ever I become a queen," muttered the princess as she journeyed into nowhere, each step as heavy as a mountain, as steep as a trench, "I shall never send hapless young courtiers on unreasonable quests simply to gratify my vanity. I like the quest, yes, as much as the next person—a quest to gain glory, regain honor, that's worth something. But risking life and limb that's not even yours in order to have a grand suit of clothes, however unique it may be, is not a very noble attitude."

She went on, nevertheless, since it was her head at risk if she did not bring the cloth back with her and her life about to evaporate into a soul if the ghoul got to her before she got to it.

She traveled on through green meadows and dusty plains, through high mountains and running rivers, through thick jungles and sterile stretches, where nothing but scraggy scrub grew a bit, then could grow no more because it became entangled and impaled on itself.

"Like my own life," she thought, "which seems to be coiling in and around on itself instead of outward and on."

But she never stopped longer than the journey of a night owl or the circling of an afternoon eagle. And finally she reached a town where she heard something of interest from two women who were baking bread by a large oven and crying their eyes out while they did it.

They heaved a tray of loaves into the fiery mouth of a huge square oven, then retreated a moment, sobbed, slapping each other's shoulders, mourning, lamenting. Then on to the next batch of bread. They were baking up a desert summer, those two women, then raining down a monsoon torrent to damp it down.

"Why are you crying?" the bodyguard asked.

The women looked at her in amazement.

"You must be a stranger! Everyone in this town knows that if someone is crying it is because they have lost a loved one—or are about to."

The bodyguard frowned, then she scratched her head, then she rubbed her chin. Finally, she asked the women, "Is this a riddle or an enigma for me to solve?"

The women let out a wail that would have cracked the heart of an ice mountain, shattered glass, made the trees wither.

"We have no heart for riddling," the mother lamented. "But you must be a stranger. You clearly don't know that on the first day of every week an ogre comes to this city demanding two hundred pieces of bread, a goat, and a human. Tonight my son is to be that human."

"What is your king doing about this terrible problem?"

The daughter's eyes were red and sore and swollen as she gurgled out her reply from deep within her sobs.

"The king has decreed that anyone who can get rid of the ogre will receive half his kingdom and the hand of his daughter."

Wahda put her arm around the mother.

"Dry your tears," she said. "Your son is safe. I will take his place in the ogre's hamper tonight."

"But why? No one gives his life for someone else's," gasped the mother. "Why should you?"

"You're right, Mother. No one gives up his life for another, and I am no different."

Wahda had no intention at all of dying. She wanted to win that half-kingdom that was on offer because always at the back of her mind, you see, was the longing to find her family. Half a kingdom meant half its army and half its resources and half a lifetime closer to being able to find her husband. There was, of course, the small matter of the princess who was to be her bride, but no doubt when the two met they would find a solution.

So the bodyguard presented herself to the king and stated her intention to replace the young man who had been put on the menu for the ogre's weekly supper. The king, of course, was overjoyed and agreed at once. If a life was saved, it was all to the good, and if that life belonged to one of his subjects, all the better. Then Wahda returned to the old woman, who was now a different person, all cuddles and kisses and blessings and her daughter all smiles and guiles and flirtation—because, don't forget, she thought Wahda was a young man. What a well-favored young man and how brave and big-hearted! And the bodyguard, princess, stranger, had a wonderful evening, at the end of which she asked the old woman to lead her to the spot where the ogre's picnic was to be placed.

The two set off, trudging along, pushing their cart as night fell and shadows lengthened and houses changed into trees and roads into footpaths and footpaths into dust, through the gates and outside the walls of the city and still farther, to the top of a small hill. And there at the top of the hill was an old, derelict shack and on one side of the shack Wahda tied the goat and surrounded it with bread. On the other side she placed a log and painted it. She gave it a face and dressed it in clothes and even wound the long fabric of her own turban around its head. Then, with a jaunty air, she tilted the turban forward to make it look as if the victim had fallen asleep.

When she turned around to see if the old woman was admiring her handiwork, she found her gone.

"No wonder," she thought, amused. "The ogre's probably due any moment."

She dug herself a pit and hid in it.

It was dark by then and in the pit even darker, which made Wahda feel safer. And there were many noises and tremors and movements that kept her alert from fear as she crouched there with her sword held ready. Midnight came and with it a feeling of chilling eeriness, but the bodyguard kept her head erect and her hand poised. Then out of the blue came a horrendous roar and the hillside shook as thunderous footsteps rushed up it and into the hut.

The ogre—he was here. He had the shape and form of an enormous, ugly man covered all over in coarse, dark hair, straggly and mangy like a diseased wolf. And how he guzzled that bread and how he ripped apart that goat, drooling at the mouth and swallowing with such frenzied morsels that his throat heaved and produced a creaking sound every time. Wahda was quite overcome with disgust. But that was the princess in her and with great determination she summoned back the bodyguard. She kept her eyes fixed on the ogre. Watching. Watching and waiting.

The ogre swallowed the last of the goat, his sinews and his bones, his hooves and his horns, his testicles and his eyes . . . there was not the tiniest fluff of fur for the wind to waft away. He stretched and yawned and a great spray of saliva issued from his throat like a sudden cloudburst. Then all at once he roared again, rushed at the log, and grabbed it, insatiable. Slash! An arm jerked, a sword glinted, a leg was sliced. The ogre's. For exactly at the right moment the bodyguard had attacked the ogre and accomplished her mission.

Oh, what a clamor the ogre set up and what a howl trailed behind him and spread, echoing and re-echoing around the countryside as he hopped on his one good leg from the hut to the distant hills where he lived!

The feasting and celebrating lasted several days in the city when the bodyguard returned and presented the ogre's leg to the king. Then she was introduced to the princess she was to marry.

"When I was a young child," began the bodyguard, "I often heard stories about kings and in those stories there were kings just like your father, who offered their daughter's hand in marriage in return for some difficult mission. I always wondered when I heard those stories what the princess herself thought of being turned into a reward to be given away at the whim of her father?"

"I can't speak for others," replied the reward, "but a princess is brought up to do what is best for her father and his subjects. My father has offered me as the reward for getting rid of the ogre and restoring safety and happiness to my people and I will honor his word."

"But surely you worry about this suitor? Will he be rough

and uncouth? Will he be a villain? Could it possibly even be a woman in disguise?''

At these last words the princess's eyes filled with tears and she spoke without thinking.

"Oh, then my dreams would come true," she wept, "because I would embrace her and call her my sister and tell her that I am very much in love with one of my father's courtiers. But I have never told my father about my lover. He pledged me as the prize for getting rid of the ogre when I was only twelve and I knew duty came before desire."

"In that case, call me sister!" commanded Wahda. "I am a woman disguised as a man. I will tell the king that I should have the right to marry you to anyone I choose."

Accordingly she told the king that she was already married and would find a suitable match for the princess. However, she had a mission of her own and would return when, God willing, she had achieved it. At first the king argued: "Men can marry as often as they like. Even more so if they are kings."

But the bodyguard insisted that she could not marry again, and in the end the king agreed.

"On condition," he insisted, "that this marriage takes place elsewhere so that my subjects do not think their princess has been rejected."

Wahda agreed and set off on her quest to find the cloth for her king so that he could give it to his queen.

Days turned into weeks, weeks into months, months into a quarter, a half, three-quarters of a year—a year, a night, and a morning—before the bodyguard, the princess, the stranger, the hero, the half-king came to a fortress in the wilds. A fortress and a wilderness that somehow felt full of magic, miracles, and missions on the verge of being fulfilled.

It was a bleak castle, an ugly castle even, and it seemed to wear a frown and a formidable look and a challenging attitude. But the gates were open and our hero walked through them into a large courtyard. There, in a silence that magnified every whisper of a breath, every click, every shiver, sat a young woman. Alone. Alone, and engrossed in her spinning—but not so engrossed she didn't hear the magnified sounds of a stranger entering her castle.

But what was this? The girl was reacting very strangely to the bodyguard's arrival, for first she laughed, a tinkling, twinkling, silver laugh, then she sobbed, a heaving, racking, wrenching sob.

"Why are you laughing and crying at the same time?" asked our hero, perplexed.

"I'm laughing at my good fortune and crying for your bad fortune," replied the young woman. "I'm lucky to be seeing a human at last. My foster parents, you see, are ghouls. They will be home soon and I'm crying because they will eat you as soon as they see you."

"Can't I get away?" Wahda asked, always quick, ever resourceful and mindful of her safety. "There must be somewhere I can hide in this enormous fort without being found."

The maiden shook her head doubtfully, thinking hard. "It's all in the smell, you see. They sniff people out. But maybe I can throw them off your scent. Just for one night, then. Come with me."

So up she stood, a spring in her feet, a new ring in her laughter, a smile in her eye and such mischief in her smile that would bring a laugh to the stoniest heart. She chattered gaily as they went, enlivening the mournful corridors, lightening up the heavy doors as they swung back and forth on their creaking, heaving joints. She showed him rooms as they went, filled with gems and precious metals, with bolts of silk and satin and brocade and every treasure within the knowledge of humans and others besides, for hoarding treasures is an obsession of all ogres.

At last they came to a remote, enclosed part of the castle, and the maiden stopped and unbolted a door.

"Here you are," she told him, "I'm sure you'll be safe here. At least for tonight. Though if it were up to me, I'd keep you here for ever."

By now Wahda was used to having women fawn on her—and she thought nothing of the maiden's caressing looks and loving words as she brought her food and drink and sat adoringly by as she ate. And as they spoke, the day grew older and darker and turned into night. The maiden said good-bye and left Wahda, who immediately curled into a ball and went to sleep.

Shadows twisted and with it the heart of the poor maiden who had been the captive of the ogre couple. They loved her, she knew, but life was so lonely, so miserable without other humans for company that she longed to leave this place and live with her own kind though they lavished gifts on her and in their way, yes, love. Look at them now. They unload the bags on their back and let loose some goats and chickens and the half-eaten carcass of a human. She shudders as she looks at its mutilated neck, its bulging eyes. Another hanged corpse, no doubt. O horror! O revulsion! Skin all mottled and the stench so vile and putrid she retches, pinches her nose, and clenches her eyes.

No wonder, then, that she thought the bodyguard so beautiful. She had come to think of humans as blood-smeared creatures with swollen, maimed faces and fetid skins. In fact she wondered often, as she looked at her own smooth skin and her sparkling, dark eyes so like those of a deer, if she was a freak and not like her fellow human beings at all. But then out of some dim, distant days in the past, she would remember a soft, dark woman, hair flowing around her as she suckled her with satin breasts, a man talking to her in a low, gentle voice as the woman sang songs and walked around the room. And as she moved, so the baby's eyes moved with her, like a pendulum, swaying here and there, without choice. Those same baby's eyes, wide and round and full of her parents, were now the shape of a doe's and still carried the pictures of her parents. Where were they? she wondered. Did they still miss her? Sometimes when those questions filled her mind she could hear screams of fear and fury, then sobs, impotent, helpless sobs, then the silence of distance and loss. Finally all around her sterility and stone walls and the stench of the spoils of ogres.

In those moments the maiden hated her foster parents, though she had to admit that in their way they did love her. It was, after all, the twinkle in her infant eyes and the sudden twitches and jerks of clenched fist and mischievous mouth that had softened their carnivorous hearts and made them decide to keep her for a daughter rather than devour her on the spot.

She wondered now, as she did so many times each day, if she would ever see any place other than this barren, rocky castle and its horrible confines. The sight of those two eating their loathsome meal made her shudder—all the more because the thought that they might eat her bodyguard was too much to bear. To imagine him maimed and mutilated like today's corpse, neck ripped, eyes bulging . . . Ohhh. She couldn't bear it.

Their wine smelled of blood to her that night as she saw them grow merrier and merrier before they grew maudlin.

"Our daughter is a lovely girl," said the ogre, "I was noticing how beautiful she has become."

"Ah, yes," replied his wife, "but she's not a girl anymore. She's a young woman."

"A young woman?" he responded, heaving himself up to have a look. "I suppose she is, now that I look at her."

"A woman," concurred the ogress.

"Then she must be married," stated the ogre.

The ogress nodded. "I agree. But where will we find her a husband?"

"And who would be good enough for her?" said the ogre gloomily, attempting to pour a keg of wine down his throat and sloshing it everywhere.

"No one," replied the ogress.

"Unless," declared the ogre, drooling and dripping wine-mixed saliva all over himself. "Unless I can find the man who took my leg. He's the bravest man I ever came across. I'd know him anywhere. He would make our daughter a perfect husband."

"Better the man who ripped my dress," argued the ogress. "He was braver. He had presence of mind, besides. After all, he had seen me seize the neck and drink the blood of that hanging corpse. That's more than most humans can stomach. I carry his picture in my eyes like the snake's eye carries the picture of its killer for its mate to see. If ever I see him again I'll flee like a wisp in a strong wind."

"My man was the braver," insisted the ogre.

"Mine. And quick-witted, besides."

"Mine. I'm bigger than you. Mine was braver and stronger."

"You may be bigger but I'm swifter."

"Don't talk to me about swiftness. Swiftness was in the stroke of my attacker. Like a spark was his sword. Like a prick."

"That's all you ever think of," screamed the ogress. "Your prick!"

The ogre looked baffled.

"That's what it boils down to," she continued. "You always have to be right. Because you're bigger than I am and because you've got a prick."

"But it wasn't my prick I was talking about . . ."

"Oh, really? Don't you have one? Was it your prick he cut off?"

"Now, look here!" roared the ogre, becoming more and more confused and enraged. "I said nothing about a prick. Mine or anyone else's."

"So I'm a liar, then, am I?"

With those words she hurled herself at him, screaming and tearing, a terrifying typhoon, all hair and nails and teeth, the two of them rolling about the floor, pots crashing, furniture smashing, doors banging, metal clanging until they both fell into a deep faint. Who knows which went first, but it wasn't long before the next one followed and all became blessedly quiet.

Then the maiden crept into her bed and dreamed all night about the ravishing bodyguard and how she would try and persuade him to take her with him when he went. What dreams she dreamed that night. What fantasies she fantasized. What hopes she hoped.

The next morning, when the two ogres left the house on

their bloody and predatory travels, she hurried to the body-guard's room, invited him out, and cooked him a delicious meal, talking all the time about what had gone on the previous night and how the ogre husband and wife had quarreled and fought as they chose a suitor for her.

"He sounds like a very brave and clever man," she conceded at the end of her account, "but I don't know if they'll ever find him. Besides"—and her eyes were coy and her smile seductive and her manner melting as she made her proposal—"I would much rather marry you."

"Then it shall be as you all want," declared the body-guard, continuing as she looked at the wide-eyed maid. "Because I am the one who cut the ogress's coat and severed the ogre's leg. In fact, if it weren't for the cloth of her coat, I would not be here at all."

She told the maiden the story from the first howl of the ogress to her arrival there. Well, the girl was so happy she tra-la-laad and tiddly-um-tummed for the rest of the day, cleaning and tidying and shining and polishing and waxing the castle until it twinkled and sparkled and made the ogres wonder if it was their own home they were coming back to or some strange beacon light that shone where their home had been just that morning when they left.

They looked at each other, then at the castle, then at the rest of their surroundings. Then they looked at each other again and nodded. Yes, this was certainly the same place in which they had left their castle that morning. So they marched up to the castle, and what do they hear but their silent little, somber little foster daughter singing and laughing and what do they see but that dull little, dozy little maid doing a little dance of joy.

"What can have come over her?" inquired the ogress. "I've never seen her like that. She's usually rather serious and somber. I've never heard her laugh or sing."

"You're right," agreed the ogre. "She's rather dull and usually quite dozy and I've never before seen her dance."

So they both rushed in and asked her immediately what it was that had made such a difference to her.

"Your decision to get me married," she chirped gaily.

Their chins sank to the earth and their gloom thickened the air.

"But where," they chorused, "are we to find either of those men? We've been back to where we encountered them and we've peered into a lot of faces but we didn't see the heads belonging to either of those two brave men on anyone's body."

"Do you think the same man could have been responsible for both deeds?" asked the young woman boldly.

"Could be, I suppose," replied the female ogre, frowning.

"It makes sense," agreed her husband. "After all, there aren't that many brave men about."

"And if I find him, you'll let me marry him?" demanded the woman.

"Of course," chorused the two ogres. "That's why we've been looking everywhere for him, isn't it?"

"You promise not to kill him if I bring him to you?" insisted the maid.

"Well, of course!" repeated the ogres, becoming impatient. "But how will you find him?"

"Wait here," caroled the woman, and flew up to the secret chamber on winged feet. She paused at the door before taking Wahda in. She was not going to chance losing her one ticket out of this mausoleum of her hopes, her one chance to step out of the gloom and doom of darkness and into the hurry and flurry of the world of humans.

"You promised not to hurt him," she reminded them, popping her head around the corner as an extra precaution.

The ogres nodded and put their hands to their hearts.

"Upon our eyes and our heads," they said, which the maid remembered as a phrase of welcoming and cherishing from those faded pages of her mother and father days. Her eyes suddenly filled with tears at the memory and she wiped them away quickly before turning to the bodyguard and taking him by the hand.

"Come with me," she said firmly. "All will be well." And with a flourish she presented her handsome suitor to the ogres.

"Here he is," she trilled. "The man you were both looking for."

"Ohhh!" the ogre applauded.

And "Ahhh!" his wife sighed.

Then, "How did you find him?" they both exploded.

"You promised," warned the maiden.

"Of course," agreed the ogress. "But at least let the young man tell us how he cut off a piece of my skirt."

"And how he slashed off my leg," added the ogre. "And let us eat while we talk."

"Some sweets first," said the young woman hastily in case the ogres decided to offer their guest an unholy meal of human parts, "and while you sweeten your mouth and this hero tells you everything you want to know, I'll prepare us a meal fit for kings."

"Sweeten your mouth," concurred the ogres, forcing themselves to observe the bizarre human custom of sweetening auspicious occasions with candies and halvas and sweet milk puddings. They would have preferred the delicious brains of a goat, served up in the cup of its own head, slimy and bloody and entirely in its natural state. The human practice of cooking and mixing and adding foliage and seeds to food had always been bizarre to them, but since it was the only way their foster daughter would eat, they allowed her to continue. Perhaps she was right, the hero would prefer her kind of food to theirs.

So the maiden cooked and the princess, bodyguard, half-king, hero, ogre's prospective son-in-law gave them her account of each encounter and how she had outdone them. They listened in awe, their great ogre eyelids flapping and widening as the bodyguard stood up and flew about, stooping and stretching to demonstrate exactly how she had achieved each feat. Never had the ogres seen such a spectacle. They were enthralled by this bold, buoyant, bewitching beau they had found for their daughter.

The maiden produced a meal so lip-smackingly delicious that everyone ate in silence save for the slurping and the "mmms" and the "ahhs" and the comments of culinary ecstasy. Then, when it was finished, the ogres and the bodyguard got to discussing their daughter's dowry.

"Marriage ceremony we have none," declared the ogres, "so take her and do what you want in your own way. But we've rooms and rooms filled with jewels and precious metals and every delight that has ever been savored by the human or supernatural mind. So let our daughter take you for a tour around the castle and choose whatever you want."

"I've seen most of what you have in those rooms," replied the bodyguard, "and it's up to your daughter what she wants to take because I have riches enough of my own. But when I returned to the king after that meeting at the gibbet, I gave him the piece of cloth I had cut off your skirt. He gave it to the queen, who liked it so much she wanted a suit of clothes from it. All I want for myself is a bolt of that fabric."

A great grin spread across the face of the ogress.

"I have plenty of it," she slavered. "You may have it. I like the idea of a queen wearing the same clothes as me."

So the details of their departure were arranged and the bodyguard was sent to the young woman's room so that they could spend the night together before leaving the next morning.

She was a little nervous as she entered, of breaking the news to the young woman expecting to marry her soon, that she was a woman.

"How foolish," she admonished herself as she walked in. "I've cut the cloth off a demoness's skirt, I've severed the leg of an ogre, I've traveled through jungles and deserts, I've told a king's daughter this very thing and found a very fortunate solution—I've no need to fear an innocent maiden who doesn't even remember much about humans and their ways."

The young woman was waiting for Wahda decked in gorgeous clothes and jewels from top to toe, glittering and shimmering like a cluster of stars in the dark night. When she saw her future husband enter, she rose slowly from her bed, walked over, and threw her arms around his neck. And how sweetly she tilted her mouth up to be kissed. The bodyguard looked down, saw her closed eyes, her upturned face, and felt a rush inside her of all the dormant passion, the unsatisfied yearning she had endured since her husband had abandoned her. How she had yearned for his arms around her, his body in her bed—but no, she must be honest with the young woman.

She dropped a gentle kiss on her lips, then squared her shoulders and stepped back with determination. The young woman looked up, disappointed.

"I think we should sit down and talk," said the princess.

The young woman was bewildered. "Have I done something wrong?" she said in a rush. "I'm not sure how people behave. I mean, I haven't lived with them for such a long time—in fact never . . ."

"No, no, no," the princess comforted her, "you've behaved just as any new bride should. There's nothing wrong with your instincts at all."

"Then why did you back away from me?"

The princess laughed. "Any man worth his salt would be delighted with you. It is just"—she took a deep breath and held the young woman's hand tightly—"I am not a man. I am a woman, just like you. I dress as a man because the world out there—the human world, as you call it—is not actually terribly safe for women on their own."

And she told the young woman the story of her father-in-law, how fate decreed that he lose his kingdom and how she and her sister had been abandoned by their husbands and their parents.

Well, the young woman was desolate to find that the young man she had dreamed of all her life, who would come and rescue her and take her with pomp and ceremony into the human world, had turned out to be a woman.

"But I feel what I feel," she declared, "whether you are a man or a woman."

"Well," replied the princess thoughtfully, "I've suspected for a long time that men can love men and women can love women in the same way as husbands and wives love each other.

And I've often worried that my employer, the king, has taken a fancy to me though he thinks I'm a man. I'm sure that's the reason his wife the queen has sent me on this difficult journey."

Women falling in love with women dressed as men, men falling in love with women dressed as men—the poor young woman did not know where she was! So she agreed to keep the princess's identity a secret and go back with her to her kingdom. There she would have the pick of partners to choose from, for the world was divided into the zenana, ruled and inhabited entirely by women, and the world of men into which they occasionally ventured.

So they left the next morning as planned, with a coach and horses and carts carrying jewels and treasures untold and stopped at last when they arrived at the kingdom where she had severed the leg of the ogre.

This time the city had a different atmosphere. People laughed and joked and went about their business singing and humming and whistling. The bodyguard made her way to the king's palace, said she had accomplished her mission and was ready to return home with the princess.

"I will leave my half of the kingdom in your care," she told the king, "and in trust for your daughter. But I may need your help, and if I do, I will ask for your military alliance."

The king was delighted that his kingdom would not be cut in half and promised all the help the bodyguard needed. So she and the princess left the castle happily and along the way collected the princess's lover and made their way back to Wahda's employer.

There was a wonderful welcome waiting for them and when the princess, bodyguard, returning hero presented the king with the bolt of cloth, he was so excited and relieved to see his bodyguard back with his mission accomplished that he promoted the princess to the position of prime minister.

The prime minister's first job was to arrange the marriage of the princess to her lover and find him an appropriate post at court. Then she turned her mind to the young woman who had been brought up by the ogres. She was harder to please. Every handsome young man she saw became her ideal mate until another even more enchanting came along. Then there were the women, so captivatingly clever, so gentle and full of fun—she decided she would wait until one person enchanted her more than all the others and she could settle for him. So she lived with the two princesses in their mansion and spent her time learning human ways—how to delude the censorious and trick the wicked and fulfill her fantasies. And soon the prime minister gave up trying to arrange a match for her and concentrated on trying to find her own family and protect herself from the advances of the king and the jealousy of the queen.

She sent messengers and spies far and wide, but no one could find any trace of the king her father-in-law, or his family.

"It is understandable," she thought, "because they have probably changed their names so that no one will recognize them. That's the usual way of deposed kings."

But she continued to worry about them, for qualified kings and princes cannot do very much apart from hunting and meeting other kings and ruling—most of all ruling—and what good is ruling if you haven't a country to rule over anymore? So she got to thinking and came up with a proposal that might well get the results she wanted.

"Your Majesty," she told the king one day, "I think it would be a wonderful idea to set aside a large area of the kingdom to grow the rarest and most exotic plants from all over the world."

At the back of the plan was the thought that people would come from far and wide to bring unusual flora and fauna to plant in her garden, including the poor and the unemployed, who could forage for them in forests and in the wilds. And among them could be her husband.

"We can send messengers to all the kingdoms around and spread the word far and wide that we will reward anyone who brings us an unusual plant."

"Excellent!" said the king, and ordered a vast area of land to be set aside for the purpose.

The prime minister ordered her messengers to spread the news and soon travelers began to stop as regularly at the new garden as merchants stop at palaces and pilgrims at places of worship. The two princesses brought in the best painters and commissioned paintings of the four members of their family, instructing them about every detail, every facial mannerism, every quirk and expression. And when the artists had completed their work they ordered the portraits to be hung up at every meeting point so that each visitor could be watched and vetted by their staff. And anyone who could possibly have been the owner of one of those faces on the wall was presented personally to one or other of the princesses, who would engage them in conversation and peer into their faces to see if they could recognize them after all this time. But neither their husbands nor the king and queen ever visited their mansion.

The weeks turned into months, the months into years— one, two, three. Ah! Three's the lucky one, they say—but no, it was the fourth year. Four whole long years after the garden was created, four people arrived—one for each year—with a small collection of plants. And what a ragtag little bunch they were as they lined up to present their offerings and collect the reward. There was an old man: he was bent and his head hung down on his chest. There was a woman who was old and wrinkled and frayed but held her head high and her back straight—head as high and back as straight as a queen. A strange sight on a beggar, but there it was. And with them, you've guessed it, were two men. Young or not, you couldn't really tell because their faces were ravaged with grief and their locks, as wild as their eyes, coursing past their shoulders, matted, joining with their beards.

There was something about the quartet, something indefinable, something that smacked of princeliness, of kingliness and certainly of queenliness that made the gardener ask if they would wait and see the head gardener, the head gardener asked them to see the majordomo, the majordomo served them with a splendid meal and asked them to rest in the guest house while he went in search of the prime minister. And all this worried the four visitors.

"What's going on?" asked the old man when the majordomo had gone. "Where are we? Are we being held prisoners? I can hear people come and go—why don't you pay us so that we can go on our way?"

You see, the king could not see how well they had been treated because he had wept so much from guilt and from shame for abandoning the two princesses that he had become blind. So his wife described his surroundings to him and comforted him. The young men had been past speaking for years because every time they opened their mouths a recrimination burst out, or abuse or grief.

"It is a punishment for the terrible thing we did," ranted

the king. Every time they failed, everything bad they experienced, everyone who reviled them the king attributed to his crass and merciless act all those years ago.

"I never realized when that witch told me I would lose everything that she was including my dignity, my nobility, every shred of virtue I'd ever had." And the king sobbed again as he had sobbed nearly every day since that first day. He imagined the young girls, their tender skins torn by cankers and thorns as they waded through the jungle, their delicate faces lacerated, their bodies shredded limb from limb by wild animals. The queen had her thoughts too. Of other kinds of animals. Ones who wore clothes and shaved their faces and had the manner of civilized beings but nurtured within themselves the worst of the animal kingdom and preyed on women in the most horrible, the most unforgivable, the most destructive ways. She shuddered. Her sons shut their eyes and they all retreated into their respective worlds of silence and seclusion.

They remained in those silent worlds of guilt and shame and sorrow and despair until finally the majordomo located the princess, who sent for the prime minister. Together Wahda and Sughra went to inspect the visitors who had been kept waiting for so long.

"I hope you are comfortable," the prime minister declared, entering the room with Sughra hovering behind, her veil drawn across her cheek. "I am sorry you have had to wait. I came as soon as I heard you were here."

"We're quite comfortable enough," replied the queen, and the stateliness of her posture, the poise of her manner, the delicacy of her voice, sent a shudder of expectation through the princess and the prime minister. "But we have not been told why we are being detained."

220 . Handsome Heroines

A touch of haughtiness in her voice here, and how the young women reveled in the hope it brought! But that face, that wizened, faded skin, the withered blooms of lip and eye—that was not a face they knew. And the men—the bent, gnarled tree-stump of a father, the feral, mute youths, not more than a step away from the animals of the jungle. The sisters looked at each other and slowly shook their heads, their hearts, oh, so heavy with disappointment. These were not the people they were looking for. But disappointment had become easier and easier to bear as the years had worn on; hope harder and harder to hold on to.

"My sister and I hope you will stay to another meal," the prime minister said, turning to leave, though something was teasing away at her mind, tugging away at the part of her memory that recognized shapes and movements and other indefinable things. "Thank you for your selection of plants. You will receive your payment after you have eaten."

Then one of the men stepped forward, holding up his hand. The prime minister's heart stopped and she froze to the spot. It was the hand! The hand that she recognized, the slender, beautiful hand of her husband. His hands had retained their shape though the skin was roughened and callused. Then other aspects of the appearance of the four visitors began to form into the shapes and the colors and the textures of people she had loved and missed. Her mind and her eye worked swiftly together, converting the tattered rags to rich clothes, the matted locks to silken ones, removing the wildness of expression and the drooping misery of their unhappy frames. And what she saw was her husband and his family.

What a miraculous metamorphosis! What a stirring transformation! Years and years of trial, of waiting and hoping, of grieving with a smile on her face—of covering her limbs in the clothes of a man and clothing her manners in the cloak of a man—all suddenly rewarded.

The prime minister turned briskly away, though it tore at her heart to ignore her husband's signal after all these years. But the part of her that had been angry with him for so long felt honor was satisfied when she saw the grief and the wildness of him and wondered if, after all, it would be easier to forgive him than she had thought.

She ran all the way to her room, Sughra behind her, until they were safely inside it with the doors locked. Then they fell into each other's arms and wept and discussed what their next step would be.

"Well, first of all," said the princess sensibly, "let us make sure they are not served a meal until we are ready. And if they insist on leaving, someone will follow them. I will send them each a set of new clothes and attendants to bathe and change them. That will delay them awhile."

When she had left to make the necessary arrangements, the prime minister stood in front of the mirror and took a long look at herself. How convincing she was as a man! A very young and quite effeminate man, but nevertheless a man. She had learned to hold her arms slightly away from the shoulder to claim more space around her body. Her step had lengthened to a stride, and as she stood, her legs were planted farther apart than they had ever been when she dressed as a woman. As she reached her arms up to undo her turban, she paused and looked at herself for the last time as a man. And she felt a twinge of wistfulness. This guise had served her well. Manhood had served her well. She had risen from the wife of a prince to the owner of half a kingdom, a demon-slaying hero, a prime minister.

Then the question struck her: would she ever have known what she could achieve if old woman What-will-be-will-be had not visited her father-in-law? She resolved then and there that she would never return to the position of merely a wife. A wife would never be a "mere" thing in her kingdom, a dispensable creature to be taken to bed and abandoned sleeping in that bed when fortunes changed.

With a flick of her wrist, she tugged at the trailing end of her turban and down it tumbled, winding, twisting with tendrils of hair whirling and twirling as she unbound herself and danced around the room with joy. Then, sobering up a little, she took off each garment and put it ruefully away.

When she emerged from her bath, she found a set of clothes in a silver tray on her bed.

"These have been waiting for the day when I would have my sister back," said Sughra, helping her to dress. And they laughed a little when the prime minister fumbled slightly, out of the habit of swathing her breasts in yards of silk and decking her hair with twinkling ornaments.

When Wahda was dressed again, the two sisters made their way to their guests. This time all six looked at each other and each recognized the others, though the two princes and their parents were too amazed and too ashamed to say much. The princesses on the other hand explained what had happened to them and plied them with food and drink and goodness and questions and by the time the night was over they had all been reunited and had caught up with a great deal about each other.

In the morning the prime minister made her way to the

king's chamber. A vast cloak covered her woman's clothes and a piece of cloth her hair. Without a word, she signaled the King's attendants from the room, bowed deeply before him, then stood up again and dropped the cloak.

"Now, Your Majesty," she declared, "I no longer have any secrets from you."

Well, the king was beside himself with a flurry of different emotions and thoughts and questions. What was happening? How had she concealed her true self for so long? Who was she? Why was she disguised?

"Most important, Your Majesty," the prime minister reminded the king in order to ensure her own safety, "I have loved you and served you well, your kingdom has prospered under my instruction, and you have been pleased with my efforts."

The king acknowledged that all this was true, and then Wahda sat down beside him and told him her story.

"And now that I have found my husband and his family," she ended, "I have a request to make."

"What is it?"

"Your Majesty, I would like you to give me an army so that I can win back the kingdom we lost."

"Granted!" beamed the king.

So the army was made ready and the prime minister sent a messenger to the other king to fulfill his promise of lending her his army.

Then the prime minister rode out at the head of the troops with her husband on one side and her brother-in-law on the other.

The Coward
and the Heroine

A little bit here, a little bit there and it mounts up soon enough; drop by drop rivers are formed, dinero by dinero a fortune is collected, brick by brick a mansion is built. And so it was with Maria Teresa's husband. A little word here, a little anecdote there, and his reputation soon built up. All those tales so delicately balanced, so sensitively formed that his bragging did not sound like bragging at all—just a good yarn.

Maria Teresa had to admit it was no more than a little bit here and a little bit there, but since all his patrons consisted of the rich—caballeros, courtiers, noblemen, and the like—it was not surprising that the king himself had come to hear of the brave exploits of this young tailor. So they flocked to him from all over Zaragoza, not merely to be dressed by him, but to hear accounts of his bravery. Now his fame was spreading outside Zaragoza to other parts of Aragon, God save us.

"He thinks he's like that other one," grumbled Teresa, "the one in the story who killed seven flies and made everyone think he'd dealt with seven men—even seven giants."

And it was indeed astounding how swiftly the children in Juan's stories turned into men, the men into giants, the giants into armies of demons. One day, she was sure, he would boast of defeating old Nick himself, and where would that leave him in the scramble to get to St. Peter rather than the devil? Lies were, after all, the devil's currency, and every God-fearing person knew it.

Maria Teresa's soul flinched when she heard Juan telling a customer about their encounter with some children on the way back from the market on the outskirts of Zaragoza. Poor, starving souls—one had tried to snatch some bread from her basket, and when Juan set upon him with his smart staff, the others tried to drag the beggar child out of reach. That was the sum total of the episode. As far as Teresa was concerned, it seemed cruel to beat a child for stealing food, though she knew he could be hanged for it. But when she told Juan he dismissed her views with what she thought was not very Christian charity. As if that were not bad enough, Juan brought the incident as naturally into his conversation as he let the stitches on his fine seams flow off the edge of the garment into invisibility.

"We need the pockets firm at the top and lined doubly strong," he murmured the very next day, as if to remind himself of this extra service he was offering to his clients.

"And why's that, Juan?" asked the nobleman he was fitting.

"Oh, nothing you need bother much about, sir," Juan replied, affecting surprise that the man had heard him. "They say the first sign of madness is to speak your thoughts aloud. And that is just what I was doing, my lord—speaking my thoughts aloud. So I must be on my way to lunacy. If I'm not there already."

"We can't lose you to lunacy," quipped the nobleman. "Why, you're too fine a tailor for that. Now, what was that innovation you were muttering about? Stronger pockets. Why? Is it the latest fashion?"

"Nothing like that, sir. It's just the children on the out-skirts of the capital, you see. They're always hanging around the market, lying in wait for the well-to-do." Juan hesitated as if he loathed having to speak about the matter. "They're hungry, and God knows, hunger makes beasts of us all."

"Why, man, you're not suggesting I line my pockets with coins to throw those ragamuffin *guitanos*, are you?"

"No, no, no. On the contrary, sir. I mean, they are not afraid to approach you bold as brass, palms upturned, as if beg-ging for crumbs, so innocent and so pitiful—then, while they have your attention, another of their gang races forward, snatches at your pocket, and pulls out your bag of coins. Then others set about you and"—his face filled with horror and he let go of the measuring and the molding and crossed his wrists in front of his face as if fending off something demonic—"they have sticks and spears and pointed rocks . . ." His voice faded away as if his thoughts were too unbearable to utter.

The nobleman frowned. "It seems to me that you have had some bad experience with these imps recently."

Juan nodded. "You don't want to hear about it, sir. It would be nothing to you, with your courage and skill with weapons. But I'm a tailor and the only skill I have is with a needle." He shook his head. "But how hungry they must be to turn into such wild creatures. Feral is what they are: wild, stray, and savage."

The nobleman was fascinated. "You are a strange fellow, Juan," he remarked. "I had no idea you were such an altruist. And what happened next?"

Juan shook his head sadly. "I should have liked to hand them the entire basket of shopping," he said in almost a whisper, "but my wife was with me and I could not take any risks. They were pulling and pushing at her with such viciousness that my only thought was to chase them away." His pause was full of emotion. "I struck one of them." Then his voice quickened, picking up momentum with every phrase. "Immediately they left Teresa alone and surrounded me. Which was of course my intention. They were hurling stones, prodding me with sticks. I ducked and fended them off with my hands. There must have been—oh—fifteen or more. Like a little army they were, and as strong and cunning as demons. They bit and scratched, but eventually I chased them away—thankfully, without harming a single hair on any of their poor, deprived heads. I lost my coat though. That is no longer wearable. Still, it might keep a poor man warm at night."

"Well, you'll sew yourself another soon enough," laughed the nobleman, delighted with the story. "For you're every bit as fine a tailor as you are a storyteller."

Juan bowed and postured and mumbled how ashamed he was that the great and courageous nobleman should come to hear of his disgrace. How he had been outdone by a group of beggar children. The nobleman in turn reassured him he had acquitted himself every bit as well as any musketeer and without recourse to weapons or cruelty. He was proud to know such a man.

Teresa, however, was not proud of Juan's tall tales. She did not like the lies, and even more, she disliked the way she was always the weakling, the one who needed saving, the damsel in distress. Juan knew she was perfectly capable of looking after herself, but still his stories cast her as fearful and frail-hearted while he was the chivalrous rescuer.

What about the time she had dealt with the vicious dog that had wandered into her kitchen from a neighboring village? They would have lost the week's meat if she had not fought him with her naked hands. How he bared his fangs and gnashed his teeth, eyes glowing and flashing fire, saliva sticky and plentiful as he growled and lunged, growled and lunged. But she stood in front of that joint, kicking at him even though he snapped and bit at her ankles and ripped her skirts. She could not remember to this day how she had managed to get rid of him. One moment he was tearing at her petticoats, growling and snapping, and the next he was slinking away. But that did not deter Juan. Oh, no!

The very next day she heard him relating the anecdote to a customer—only the woman had become the man, Teresa transformed to Juan, the dog was some unimaginable wild animal—maybe a tusked boar—and he had run off howling when Juan grabbed him by his tusk, practically wrenching it off. Those screams had filled Juan with mercy and he decided not to finish him off. He prayed that the wound he had given the creature would soon heal—though he could not be sure at all. Should he bring it up in confession? he asked anxiously.

Mercy me! God save him from the devil's grasp. He

smiled and bowed and renounced his actions and as usual gave the impression that he considered his deeds less than noble and that his great feats of bravery were some natural, unintentional phenomenon quite beyond his control. Boasting yet giving the impression of modesty. It was devilish.

"I did it without thinking," Juan would say apologetically, head bowed. "Maria Teresa's life was at risk. She is so fragile. If I'd had time to take it all in I'd probably have run with her for protection. But she looked so helpless standing there, turned to stone from fear."

"And just how did I look when I stood helpless, watching you rescue me from the wild boar?" demanded Teresa that night over the rescued joint.

But Juan only laughed. "Why worry?" he said reasonably. "My customer's admiration is no good to you. On the other hand, if he admires me, it will help my trade. Caballeros are impressed with bravery in those around them. They send their companions to be fitted by me."

He gestured around him. The furnishings, the size of the room, the food on the table, and the dishes that held it—everything was far above the standard of life a tailor could expect. Even a tailor to the aristocracy—a tradesman.

"All this is in no small part thanks to my reputation as a brave tailor."

"We know about brave tailors," Teresa muttered, feeling guilty for not being able to forgive him. There was a dark vapor building inside her that she could not quite explain, and if it did not melt soon, it would explode and the explosion would be directed at Juan.

Teresa crossed herself, asked sweet Jesus for guidance and

patience and absolution. She would have to confess her evil thoughts to Father Raphael. Yet she was sure Juan confessed nothing because he believed his tales were inoffensive.

"Do beggars care if they appear in stories? Do dogs suffer if they are maligned for beasts? Come, come, Teresa, get some perspective into your moral rantings. What I say harms no one."

"Perhaps not, but that doesn't stop it being a lie," insisted Teresa. "And one thing more—why do you always portray me as a coward?"

"A coward? It becomes a woman to be gentle-hearted. Don't you realize how I elevate you in my tales? My stories are concocted to turn you into a heroine to be envied by fine princesses."

"And yourself into the most valiant of knights," she returned.

Oh, the look of hurt on Juan's face! He postured and he protested that she was accusing him of vainglory. He, Juan, the man she had married and who tried to give her everything she wanted and needed and asked for and a great deal she had not even asked for. But Teresa was unmoved.

"I'd happily give it up if you stopped lying. Lying is a sin."

"It's not a lie, Teresa, it's just a bit of fun, a way of publicizing myself. This is the capital city. Tailors can be had as easily as a glass of wine. But it isn't about the sin, is it, my sweet Teresa?" he chided, his eye baleful. "It is because you want stories that make you the strong one, the brave one, the heroic one. Well, I can tell you here and now, no one wants to hear stories like that. It is unnatural for women to want praise for unwomanly acts."

"We perform these unwomanly acts every day of our lives," snarled Teresa, "and you expect us to. But you don't want to praise us for it. Nor do you want to acknowledge our bravery. Why, Juan? Do you think it might make us feel too independent? Like you stopped me from riding horses? Would it unman you to acknowledge my strength?"

"I'll admit one thing," retorted Juan. "My tongue will never be stronger than yours."

"Oh, I don't know," she said sweetly. "Mine could never launch a story as hefty as the ones you tell."

And so it went on. He told lies, she objected, he persisted, she protested. It was the only thing they never agreed on. Never. And that vapor inside Teresa, it lingered in spite of the novenas and the prayers and the confessions. Sometimes it was so intense, she was afraid the moment for the explosion had come. She recognized the vapor and she named it. Revenge. That was what she wanted. Revenge. To teach Juan such a lesson that he would never again boast his horrible boasts and demean her.

"For the moment, I'll leave it to God to punish him," she decided.

But God did no such thing. The very day after Teresa had decided to leave punishment to Him, Juan received a great honor that was the direct result of his bragging. Two of his regular patrons arrived, all smiles and back-patting and "come-inside-we've-something-very-important-to-say-to-you." Well, of course Juan asked them inside and sat them down in his parlor and ordered refreshments. He was amazed; Teresa was astonished. These men were treating Juan as an equal. What was behind it all?

Well, what was behind it was a request that Juan should carry gold and jewels worth a large amount of money from Zaragoza to Guadalajara. He would be provided with a cart and a horse and he must go alone across bandido country. Of course he would be paid well for his risks. They knew he was a brave man. The bravest they knew, bar the noblemen and caballeros, of course, and it was important that the gold should be carried by a man who looked simple and could pass as a—well—tradesman. Soldiers and guards passing the region were consistently targeted by the highwaymen. Caballeros, too, attracted undesirable attention. So if Juan went along with a chest of clothes, freshly made, he could claim a hundred reasons for traveling: trade, the possibility of moving from one city to another, extending his circle of business. The reality was, it was unlikely he would have to say anything at all. The bandits would not be interested in attacking a simple horse and cart. It would not be rich enough pickings.

Juan accepted the mission immediately, flattered by the noblemen's tributes of valor and honesty and friendship. So they left, after depositing with him the gold and diamonds and other precious gems.

Juan's head was so inflated, it was flying with him.

"Haven't you thought how risky this whole business is?" demanded Teresa.

"Now where's your strong heart?" teased Juan. "You were always the courageous one, or so you claimed. Now look at you, quivering and pale while I find myself equal to the task and not afraid at all."

"You have started to believe in your own bragging!" gasped Teresa fearfully. "And what do you think you can do against an army of bandidos, if they decide to attack you? Do you know how ruthless they can be?"

"What do bandits want with a trunkful of fancy clothes?"

asked Juan. "And if they want clothes, let them have the whole trunk. They'll never find the gold and gems."

Teresa nodded. "You must make sure the treasure is well hidden," she agreed. "Somewhere they will never think of looking."

They pondered where such a place would be. On the underside of the cart, perhaps? Maybe in the saddle? Or bridle? How about in Juan's boots? Somehow all these places seemed vulnerable. Perhaps with the food? No, bandits would probably find food interesting enough to cart away—or eat on the spot. Wine, they'd never ignore. Morning came, but Juan and Teresa were no nearer deciding where the treasure should be hidden.

"Well, we must make a start on completing and packing the clothes for your journey," said Teresa.

For the next week, they sewed and hemmed and embroidered and crocheted, smocked, frilled, and buttonholed until eventually Juan had enough clothes to fill a trunk.

"Of course you will need another box," said Teresa, "to carry your own clothes."

And then the idea struck her.

"Why don't I sew the treasure into the hems and belts of the clothes you are wearing? And you can carry a plausible sum of money in a purse and some hidden in your shoes, then, if they persist you can hand that over."

"And all the time the real treasure will be safe," said Juan smugly. "What a good idea."

So Teresa set about sewing the gems neatly and carefully into the garments, making sure there were no lumps and bumps and no excessive weight to give away their hiding place. And soon Juan was ready to leave.

"I was touched by your concern for me," he said as he kissed Teresa before leaving. "But I knew from the start that the highwaymen would never find the treasure where I intended to hide it."

"*You* were confident . . . ?" gasped Teresa. "You intended to hide it? I was the one who suggested the hiding place!"

Juan threw back his head and laughed. "Now who is imagining things and taking all the glory?" he demanded, tilting her face up by the chin and kissing her tenderly. "So it was your idea to sew the gold into my belt and seams, was it?"

"It was," insisted Teresa.

"No, Teresa," Juan said so gently that once again she was convinced he believed what he was saying. "It was you who sewed them in. The idea was mine. But never mind. I can see why you came to think it was yours. You worked so hard on it— and wondered while you were sewing why you had not thought of it."

Teresa held her tongue. Juan was leaving. It was by all accounts a difficult journey. She would not fight with him before he left. So she kissed and embraced him and said a prayer for his safety. And after he had gone, she went straight into his workroom and cast about for some suitable clothes. She found a pair of blue britches, a frilly shirt, a velvet jacket. Each garment was sewn with such care that the stitches melted into the fabric, the seams disappeared into the air. The turn of the hem was as debonair as a courtier twirling his lady in a dance, the frill as coquettish and alluring as the lady herself. Oh, the richness of palaces, the rhythm and melody of master musicians, the grace of the fairies—Juan the tailor's creations evoked them all. And yet he felt he needed to lie to gain work and reputation, claimed rough and violent acts for hands that could produce clothes fit not only for Ferdinand and Isabella but the gossamer people of the fairy world.

She felt a surge of anger again at Juan's parting words, at all of his lies.

"It is not a morbid suspicion," she decided. "Juan doesn't just tell tales to make himself look great, he tells them to demean me. Or why would he repeat them to me with such satisfaction?"

On a wave of anger, she hurried into the backyard carrying the grand clothes with her. She dashed them to the ground, threw mud and slops from the kitchen over them, and trampled the dirt in. Then she slashed at the coat, ripped at the frills, pulled away the buttonholes.

Oh, what pleasure! Juan's carefully prepared clothes so dirty and smelly and disgusting. His hard labor ruined. And he would have to replace the fabric and the clothes and God only knew how much it would cost him. But what ecstasy it was to plunder his glory and muddy it as he sullied hers!

With the sweetness of revenge still humming a melody inside her, she went to church. She lit a candle to the Madonna asking her to cast the eye of safety on her household and to direct St. Peter to be their guide and see them through the dangers on the road ahead.

Then she came home, pulled off her skirt, her girdle, her blouse, and bodice and climbed into the tattered remains of the britches, the shirt, and the jacket. She caught up her raven's-wing hair, all glossy and black, tied it with an old kitchen rag, and smeared it over with grease from the stove. On second thought, she would smear some of the black muck on her face too, her cheeks, her chin, and a smut on her forehead, so that no onlooker could tell which was beard and mustache, which dirt from days of riding in the wilderness. She sucked in her breath, then let it out. Whoof! She would have to get used to the stench. But it was authentic. She had heard from travelers who had encountered highwaymen that they stank of accumulated bodily excretions and stale blood and the smell went before them so far ahead that the wise and the experienced could sniff and tell when a highwayman was near.

She had to creep down to the stable in the next village to hire a horse. She chose a large fellow with a wildness about him so that when she mounted him, she felt a certain authenticity flow into her. Her back took up a different position with the determination to control him, which caused her neck to stretch to its full length and her chin to be held high and her eyebrows to be raised and in general a feeling of haughtiness to emanate from her. Oh, how good it was to be astride a horse again!

In a moment she was on the highway out of town, into a nearby village and off the beaten track. She kept sight of the highway though, so that she would not be lost, scrutinizing the road, watching, looking for the little cart and the homely pony that would at some point be trotting along the highway with its burden of jewels and gold on its way to a noble destination.

And there, at last, it came!

How small Juan looked from Teresa's high perch atop the unruly stallion and how humble and pathetic his horse and how meager and unhandsome his cart. No wonder the noblemen had felt that this humdrum method of travel would be a safe bet. Now here she was on her splendid mount bobbing and bouncing and flying free. This was power—and she could feel it. It overwhelmed her and excited her and filled her with the conviction that not a soul could stop her doing what she wanted. And now she would do it.

She dug her spurs into the sides of the horse and urged him on. Like an arrow from the bow of a master archer, he flew swift toward the road and in a few moments found his mark.

"Wheyhey!" growled Teresa, tugging firmly on his bit. "We're here."

The cart came to an abrupt halt, rattling and shuddering.

"You!" rumbled Teresa, her voice coming from her chest as it tried to grapple with the gusts of laughter that threatened to assail her.

Juan's face wore a look of terror.

"Is it your shivering that's making your cart rattle like this?"

"Your Excellency!" muttered Juan, his voice trembling, his body shaking. "Take everything, just spare my life."

"Take everything?" jeered Teresa. "What's the everything you have to offer. What are you anyway? A tinker?"

"A tailor, Your Excellency," stuttered Juan, "on my way to find new pastures. I have some wonderful clothes in the cart. You can take them."

"Dismount," commanded Teresa, enjoying herself hugely, her heart thumping with the excitement of the chase and the holdup. She had never enjoyed herself so much, even if this was a charade.

Juan stumbled off his perch and stood bowing and stooping.

"What are you waiting for?" she ordered, egging the horse on to scratch the ground and snort and scare the wits out of Juan. "Get the trunk down."

Juan obliged immediately, holding up his exquisite handiwork: britches, shirts, skirts. Teresa let out a whoop of laughter.

"And what would you suggest I do with these skirts?" she demanded. "Ride out in them? No, I fancy they'd suit you better. Put them on."

Handsome Juan—he hesitated a moment. How she longed for him to demonstrate some of that bravery he so loved to boast about. Her heart stopped. He was going to defy the highwayman. He was going to refuse to humiliate himself by putting on a skirt. Please, she urged him silently, don't do as I say. And she decided to return home without another word if he refused to do her bidding. But no, handsome Juan was turning into pretty Juanita—a little on the tall side perhaps, somewhat flat-chested—but definitely pretty. Teresa was filled with scorn.

"Undress," she commanded.

Juan shed the skirts and stood, helpless and humble.

Why is he so pathetic? she wondered. I haven't even threatened him.

"Don't hurt me, please," whined Juan.

"Why not?" she bellowed, enraged. "You have nothing else to offer me but the pleasure of a scourge and a box full of frills and ribbons."

"Please, Excellency," stammered Juan. "My clothes."

"Your *clothes*? *Your* clothes?" Teresa gaped in disbelief. He was volunteering the information. "What would I want with *your* ordinary clothes when I'm refusing the foppish ones in the box?"

"No, Excellency, I would not be so impertinent if—"

"If what?" interrupted Teresa, hoping to give Juan long enough to change his mind. But no, he had decided.

"A treasure. An absolute fortune. It's sewn into the seams, the belt." He fumbled and ripped at Teresa's fine stitches, but they did not give way.

"Your shabby old clothes, worth a fortune? I fancied you were insane. Now I see you are."

She raised her lash and Juan cowered, pulling off his shirt, undoing his belt and letting it drop to the ground so that his britches sagged around the knees.

"Put them back on!" Teresa shuddered in disgust, reaching over to the suitcase with her whip. Then she turned her horse and rode off into the distance.

Ten days later, Juan returned home. A messenger was sent to give the two noblemen news that their goods had been safely delivered and that Juan had a note to confirm receipt. Then he went to the backyard and washed himself thoroughly, dressed in fresh clothes, and sat down to a hot meal. All this while he described his journey out. How a highwayman and his horse, both wild as a hurricane, had blown up to him, accompanied by their howling companions. How they had surrounded him and threatened to kill him unless he handed over his clothes. Clearly they had known men sew money into the seams of their clothing for safekeeping. But he had stood up to them. He had folded his arms and stood in the fog of dust scratched up by their snorting, kicking horses and told them they were at liberty to take whatever they wanted, but they would not humiliate him by making him strip.

"I told them they would have to kill me before I would relinquish my dignity or the clothes on my back."

"Indeed?" cooed Teresa, wide-eyed and not a bit annoyed this time. "And what did they say?"

"To my surprise, they turned tail and rode off. I heard

their master shout I was the bravest man they had ever met and they would be better leaving before they made me really angry. He thought, you see, I was the kind of man who could demonstrate the strength of a hundred soldiers in a rage."

"Oh, Juan," murmured Teresa, "I would never have thought it. I have clearly underestimated you all these years."

"You have, Teresa," he agreed, "but I forgive you."

"So magnanimous," she said, beginning to clear away the table. "And your patrons will enjoy the story so much."

"They should be here soon," remarked Juan, looking at the clock. "And while they are, I will perfect the fitting of their new clothes."

He stood up and made toward his workroom with all the old swagger intact. Teresa watched him go, laughing inwardly. This was one lie he would not get away with. Oh, he might impress his patrons and gain their praise for getting past the bandidos and delivering the treasure, but never again would he disparage her through his bragging. She continued her work, waiting—and then it came, the bellow of dismay and frustration.

"Where are the clothes I made for Don Hernandez?"

Teresa appeared at the door, all solicitude and cooperation.

"What clothes?"

"The ones I left hanging here? Right here."

"And you're sure of that?"

"Of course I'm sure."

"I'll look down here," she said, stooping to a box at the bottom of his cupboard.

"Phssst!" Juan hissed, grabbing his nose. "Haven't you

cleaned this place recently? I'm away a week and already the place starts to stink."

"Isn't the smell familiar, Juanito?" Teresa formed her eyes into circles beneath arched eyebrows.

She lifted a bundle from the box and undid it.

"Are these the clothes you were looking for?" she asked, holding up the shredded highwayman's outfit.

"Are these the . . . have you lost your head?"

But that blue velvet. The frilled collar . . . the . . . my Lord. My Gracious Lord. He recognized it suddenly as it had looked when he left it hanging in his workroom and then again in bandido territory on the way to Guadalajara.

With a moan, Juan flung himself into a chair, his head in his hands.

"I'm not the one who lost my head," Teresa said gently. "You did. This was just my way of bringing it back to you."

"And now I suppose you'll be the storyteller? And I shall be disgraced all over Aragon."

Teresa smiled an enigmatic smile. Her revenge was complete.

A MATTER
OF HONOR

On a high peak in a remote district of Tibet, I don't know when, but in any case, very long ago, lived a young woman whose name was Nuri. And she was looking out of her window one day, waiting, harrowed with anticipation for the arrival of her future husband. He was a young man from a distant, less remote part of Tibet than this, and he was coming to marry her and live with her rich and illustrious family in the customary way. Now, Nuri knew her family had thought carefully about this man and evaluated the reports they had heard about him, and as far as they could be they were sure that he was a young man of good character and reasonable looks and would fit into the family and increase its honor. So while the house hummed with the activity of cooks cooking and mothers rushing about organizing and ordering and agonizing, as mothers do, and girls singing and dancing and playing pranks as girls do at weddings, and men thundering instructions and making their presence felt as men do on such occasions, Nuri sat by the window, just waiting.

Racked with anticipation, her two eyes were riveted to the single long, winding mountain path that led to her house. While the household cared for honor and temperament and character, at this point all Nuri cared for was how the man looked. How he carried himself, whether he was fat or thin, tall or short, light-skinned, dark-skinned—and how he would appeal to her aesthetic sense.

"No one has described him as the son of Adam," she consoled herself, for the expression "son of Adam" was a euphemism for ugly; someone who belonged to the human race but was not distinguishable in any attractive way from its less blessed members. She didn't doubt that they had made sure he was of sound mind and body, but it was possible that the finer details of his looks had not been so important to them as, for example, his temperament. After all, it was she who had to lie in the bed they made for him and live in the bed they made for her, for the rest of her life. Well, they wouldn't knowingly serve her up with someone loathsome—but the entire transaction was based on trust. Who knew what would turn up in her bag of fortune?

He was naked when he arrived. Nuri's eyes were drawn, twin flares, to his bobbing sex organ and she had to drag them away from the shame she felt for wanting to look but also because she was afraid her stare would burn him. So big! she thought, half in fear because she was a woman with narrow hips (this had been a cause of some worry to her mother: women with narrow hips were not always good child bearers) but half in pride because men with large penises were meant to be real men, masterful and capable of fathering many daughters and sons. And the more daughters the better, because daughters brought sons into the house and the more the merrier. The workforce expanded with new husbands and new sons and of course new daughters to bear and marry new sons. And so it had been for years.

By the time she tore away her eyes and burned a smoldering path from his pubis to his face, he had moved out of eye view and under the huge thatch above the door of the house. She heard the women ululate, the men laugh raucous welcome, and the girls set up a singing and a drumming and a dancing that made the walls of the house resonate and shudder with mirth and rejoicing.

Then there was a whirl of eating and more singing and dancing and laughing and chatter and finally, the two were in their bridal chamber. Nuri had managed to steal quite a few glances at her husband by this time and he was handsome. There was no doubt about it. Besides, he appeared so natural about having arrived here with no clothes on. Of course no one had said much about it, though there was some talk that he had been beset by a brigand who had turned out to be a demon. He had been lucky to escape. Clothes didn't matter much in such circumstances. They were glad he was alive.

In private, though, Nuri could not wait to get to the bottom of it, to dig out the full story behind it. She loved stories.

"Tell me," she begged, eyes all alight. "Tell me the story of the demon."

"Oh, the demon," he replied, impatient but, she fancied, a little embarrassed. "Well, this demon—this creature—was following me. When I ducked to avoid a branch, he ducked too. When I walked, he was directly behind me. When I turned, he whipped out of sight and I could feel him rise behind me."

She stared wide-eyed and full of horror. How close she had come to losing him!

"But I was too clever for him," he crowed. "I whipped off my turban and flung it over my head. That took care of him for a time. But he was back later. Following me. Oh, it went on for days."

Nuri could see he was getting impatient now. Her panting, her fearful excitement, her animation, her fragile, narrow-hipped beauty, was generating a heat in his loins, potent as the most forbidden mead, slurring his words, blurring his vision. Words, words, words. He wanted no more of them.

"Please finish your story," she pleaded, partly because she was suddenly nervous about this deflowering she had heard so much about. "Tell me how you vanquished the monster."

He moved closer. The truth was, he didn't know.

"When night fell, it disappeared. When light came, it reappeared."

He moved closer.

She sensed her maidenhead was about to be sacrificed. Blood on the sheets, the fanfare the next day as crowing, gloating women carried the tulips, her martyred virginity, on crisp white bridal sheets to be washed into the lake. Red on white, blood on snow; a sacrifice to the lake—swollen at this time of year with all those melting snowcaps to feed it. It was a wonder the waters didn't glow red during the summer months, when so many girls got married, so many tulips were washed away into the lake. She was sure there was a land of tulips, red and rubylike growing in its bed, their petals open wide, like splayed legs on the bridal bed, bearing their wounds, black and proud at the center.

He moved even closer. She could feel his breath warm on her face. It was like a soft fire, his eyes glowing embers that warmed without singeing. She throbbed, her skin felt hot.

"Then what happened?" Her voice was tremulous. It was heady, that wine of what was to come between them. She was dizzy with expectation. Yet something in her was putting it off.

"Then what happened?" There was a little fierceness in his expression, perhaps because his voice came out like a loud, urgent whisper. Then he slumped back, resigned.

"Well, I gradually threw all my clothes at it and finally it was so weakened it could do nothing. Then the night drew in, darkness was around most of the time. It was scared of the gloom, I was not. I know many prayers of protection. I chanted them, they weakened it, finally it died. I outlived it and here I am."

She fell back with a little squeal as he leaped on to her— and what a frenzy of movement. They were like a bundle, the same bundle with legs and arms and heads and loins moving frenetically, locking now, bumping now, gyrating, panting, squeaking. It went on and on, this marital game, and though she was enjoying it and the soreness was fading or at least being undermined by the pleasure, she wondered how long it would go on. Then suddenly she thought: His shadow! and the answer told her that her husband's story had been a riddle. He had been riddling all along and the answer was "A shadow!"

"Your shadow!" she screamed as a sudden rapture made her body shake and shudder—and his too, by the feel of it—and he rolled over.

Eyes glazed, voice rasping, he looked at her in exhausted disorientation. "Shadow?"

At that moment she saw the tulip slowly and richly forming in the center of the bed. Now she could begin to understand the link between martyrdom and ecstasy.

Love, she realized, was intoxicating, marriage was like an exhausting, accelerating drug: it dulled the senses and intensified the sensations. She felt some of that skin-buzzing and mind-fuzzing too. But she longed to make her mark on her new husband. Let him know how clever she was.

"Your shadow!" she persisted. "The answer to your riddle! It was your shadow following you. It appeared in the light, it emulated your movements, it disappeared in the dark. It was your shadow!"

She clapped her hands and danced about in glee, sporting her naked body and her bright mind until she realized he looked a little put out.

She sat down beside him. Perhaps women weren't supposed to dance around naked—perhaps he didn't like her guessing his riddle. He had worked so hard to camouflage the solution. No, she resolved, next time she would let him tell her the answer. And the moment she touched him, he forgot about her cleverness and how it had shown him up, and they rolled around and stirred up clouds of dust till the early hours of the morning.

As the days went by, Nuri realized that her husband was not nearly as clever or heroic as she had thought. In fact, he was a simpleton. But her hips had widened and the nights—and some stolen hours of the day—had become so pleasurable that character and courage mattered not at all. Temperament did, though, and the size of his dearly beloved "big fellow," as they both called it, was every bit as important and wonderful as everybody said. And she made sure all her girl cousins and friends knew the truth. So really, she was quite sad when that malign god Family Honor reared his ugly head and prompted her husband to decide that he would go to a big town or even a nearby country like India or China to sell goods and make some money.

"I've enjoyed myself so much these past few months," he said, "but I really must restore my honor. I have never lived down the shame of coming to your house nearly naked and without any gifts for you or your family."

"No one's said anything, have they?" Nuri asked, alarmed. "If they have, I'll deal with them. You've more than made up for it"—and here she becomes coy and her eyelids flicker and her lashes lower and create a fan to veil the desire flashing in her eyes—"you've worked hard with the family and you've made me—very happy."

"No, no," he reassures her. She sees it come to life, "big fellow," and it reminds her of the stories that some of the older women have heard from traveling Arab merchants about the "tent-pole" man whose fellow's so big, it holds up his long robe like a tent. She reaches out to fondle "big fellow." So big, yet so little and lovable and lively. But what's this? Her husband reaches out too and grasps her extended hand, clasps it lovingly to his chest, deflecting its purpose. "No—we really must talk."

She overrides him this time. His will, she realizes, is a horse that she can ride. And how she rides him and how he thrives on it, frolicking and frisking as she guides his moves and spurs him on and calls out commands.

But he kept on about his need to restore his honor until

after a few weeks she stopped and listened. He was dealing with something deep inside. Simpleton he might be, but he needed to redeem himself. To be able to hold his head up. She understood.

"These things are bigger than us," she conceded, "and a man has to do what he has to do, especially if it's a question of his honor."

And so the simpleton went, loaded with goods of the arts and crafts and dried meats of the region and carrying silver coins that he could exchange for other goods farther along. There were blue stones and red stones that the mountain people took down to the plains—though she coaxed him not to go that far—and he would do a good trade and return with his fortune and his self-respect restored.

She sat at the window and watched and waited and prayed that some plainswoman would not discover "big fellow" and keep him with her. But she need not have worried—he was back in no time at all and he returned with only the clothes he had left in. Not a bundle, not a basket, not a purse was to be seen anywhere. His head hung low, his shoulders were stooped, his eyes were great pools of humiliation.

"Well, at least it's an improvement on the last time," she comforted him. "You had all your clothes on this time."

But he would not be consoled. And horror of horrors, "big fellow" had gone into terrifying decline. Nothing would revive him. She fondled him and stroked him—even tried to breathe life back into him. Nothing worked. There was nothing left to do. She would have to get the whole story from her husband, get to the root of his misery, travel to the valley of death and snatch him back.

It broke her heart to wrench the story from him, he

looked so downcast, so wretched. But she knew it had to be done. A woman, too, had to do what she had to do. Especially if her joy was at stake.

He had stopped at an inn, he explained dully. The inn-keeper was a friendly fellow. He enjoyed company, he gladly confessed. His inn was on a quiet route and except during seasons of pilgrimage, he was lucky to meet anyone in a week.

"And it's good to talk," he said. How he could talk! He was like the steady gurgle of a volcano, preparing to erupt. And erupt he did. Into the most wonderful stories.

"It's the way of travelers," he explained. "When they're body weary they sit down for food. And when their bellies are full and the life begins to return to them, they sit by my fire. There's something about the fire—when they've been staring at it a while, they see pictures in it. Then they give words to the pictures. And I've heard many an exciting tale in my time."

He was staring at the fire himself at the time, shoving in a loaf of bread, stirring a ladle in his soup.

"But my own experiences cap those tales. I've seen many a wonder both here in my humble inn and of course when I was a traveler myself."

He never stopped fire-gazing as he spoke, and suddenly he too started to give words to the pictures he saw. Some memories, some disembodied happenings, true or untrue, no one would ever know. They came to the storyteller, the storyteller told them. It was not for him to reason why.

"And I can tell you they're all true," claimed the landlord.

His belly was full and he was happy for the company as he glared into the simpleton's eye, the fire pictures sliding through his eyeballs. "You know they're all true, don't you?"

The simpleton felt uneasy.

"What I know for a fact," he hedged, "is that they're exciting and entertaining and I don't give a jot if they're true."

The landlord brought his hand down on the table with an enormous thump. The plates and pots clattered, the spoons jumped.

"Well, that's a fine thing!" roared the landlord. "And what if I could prove the next story to you? What would you be willing to bet on it?"

"Let me hear your story first," replied the simpleton confidently.

"Then let me tell you," began the innkeeper in his story-telling voice, "that when the hills grow dark with night and the lamps need to be lit you will see a small, moving candle enter your room and light the lamp by your bed. And in the light of that lamp you will see a large black cat. Its eyes will glow and it will become obvious to you that it is no servant—for who would work in a deserted place like this? No servant, but the cat that has carried in a candle and lit your lamp. Well, would you believe that this large black cat is trained to come in and light your lamp? I've trained it myself."

The young man laughed loudly.

"Are you saying you do not believe me?" challenged the innkeeper.

"It's a wonderful tale," smirked the husband, "and it doesn't matter if it's true or not, because it's entertaining and enjoyable."

"Well, would you be willing to lay a bet on it?" snarled the innkeeper.

"I would, I would," replied the husband, thinking this was an easy way to add to his gains. "What do you want me to bet?"

252 · Handsome Heroines

"All your goods if I'm right, and my inn and everything in it if I'm wrong."

"Done!" agreed the simpleton, imagining his wife's face when he returned to tell her that the family now owned a rest house.

Well, as darkness drew in, the young man sat in his room waiting for the moment when his lamp would be lit. It grew darker and darker and he grew sleepier and sleepier, tired after his long journey and warm and lazy with his belly full of hot, nourishing soup.

"That's the trick," he thought to himself. "The innkeeper is waiting for me to fall asleep, then he'll be sure I don't see him coming in on all fours to light the candle and leave a cat in the room."

And cunningly, he pinched himself every time he felt his head nod with drowsiness, and sat up alert to wait for the lamp to be lit. At long last the door to his room opened and a small light appeared. Behind it shone two ghoulish eyes, low and so close to the ground, it could never have been the innkeeper, even if he was crawling in on his stomach. The eyes and the light moved along to the lamp on the side of his bed and lit it. And sure enough, in its glow he saw a large black cat. Oh, how his heart leaped and fell back in sorrow and shame!

"That is the truth of it," ended the husband wretchedly. "That's the story of my shame."

Well, for the first time in her life Nuri realized that family honor was truly a force to be reckoned with. And the individual who was guilty of besmirching it paid a great price. She began to notice the scorn in the eyes of her family and the sneers on their lips and the innuendo and the hidden jibes. She decided she would take this relentless deity family honor and stand him upside down with his head buried in the muck and mire of its own retribution.

"Go to my father," she instructed her husband, "and tell him you lost your fortune because you are an honest man. Tell him you want to win back your honor and ask for some more money to go out on another mission. Tell them that the inn-keeper is a great teller of tales and if you can't resolve the problem, he will make a story out of the simpleton who was accepted as a son-in-law of the family with vast properties at the top of the mountain. And there'll be tales spread to explain why such an affluent family accepted a dolt for their daughter's husband. Tales will be carried to the plains and across mountains about this daughter who has some serious defect. Her nose is too long, her temper vicious, her wits dim, her head bald. However they resist," she warned, "insist that you must act on your decision, it's a matter of family honor. And you must take me with you so that you can show me how an honorable man uses his wits to gain back his self-respect and more besides."

So the husband did as he was told and the very next day set off with Nuri, who had disguised him as an old man and herself as a young man wearing a smart beard made of the hair from the tail of an old black ram. And a slope and a half down, they arrived at the inn and she asked the innkeeper for a room.

"My father and I are on our way to visit relatives," said Nuri, "and we're carrying some precious things as gifts for them. But we need to eat and rest for the night."

Then, as the innkeeper got together the ingredients to cook his soup, Nuri scuttled about the inn and trapped three rats.

"Take these," she instructed her husband. "Do exactly as I tell you and we'll win ourselves an inn."

After the meal she told the innkeeper that her father was an old man and was very tired, so he would go to his room and sleep while she stayed up to listen to the innkeeper's stories.

As before, the innkeeper told this story and that and eventually came to the incredible tale of the cat that lit the lamps.

"Oh!" exclaimed Nuri. "What a claim and a half! I may be young and gullible, but only a fool would believe that a cat could be trained to do a thing like that."

"In that case," challenged the landlord as before, "are you willing to wager your precious goods against my inn?"

"Of course," laughed Nuri, "and an easier gain I'll never make for the rest of my life!"

The innkeeper's eyes glowed like the red coals in his furnace and the wager was struck.

Well, the night drew in and Nuri went to her room and sent her husband to wait outside by the courtyard for the cat to begin its journey. Finally, when everything was coated in darkness and the stars swathed in clouds, a small glow appeared, close to the ground as before, and began to move slowly into the courtyard. In a flash, the husband released a rat directly in the path of the cat. Its nails scratched against the stone paving as it scampered across the cat's path, glad to be freed. The cat swerved, the glow swayed, the cat steadied itself, remembering no doubt how it was beaten for its mistakes during training. Then the light steadied and the cat continued its path evenly toward Nuri's room. Another yard or two and the simpleton let loose the second rat. It skittered, it clattered across a small wooden box, distracting the cat, then crossing its path, it ran for its life. The cat's head swung in its direction, the light flickered, swayed, righted itself. The cat moved on. Another three yards or so and the third rat shot out, practically hitting the cat's nose as it went. Well, it was just too much for the cat. It dropped the handle of the tray containing the lamp, let out a raucous yowl of fury, and ran after the rat.

It was all over for the landlord, his property ownership, his tall tales, his wicked winnings—they all went to Nuri, who stood grinning and watching in the dark before she gathered herself together, and in ringing tones of irritation, demanded a light.

"Expecting me to fall asleep before you lit my lamp, were you, innkeeper?" she accused. "So that you could claim I was asleep when this wondrous cat of yours—large and black, was it—came to light my lamp? Well, I never took you for a dishonest man, though I could see you spun a thrilling yarn."

The landlord had to admit defeat but asked if he could stay on as a servant to look after the inn, and Nuri gladly agreed.

Then Nuri and her husband went to bed, and for the first time since the simpleton had lost his fortune to the innkeeper, "big fellow" came to life again.

The next day they returned home to their family in the landlord's cart drawn by a mule.

"I'm proud to say," said the simpleton to his father-in-law as he helped Nuri down, "that I've restored my honor and family honor and if you walk down a slope and half, you'll find an inn that now belongs to us and a servant to run it. And this cart and mule besides."

The family scuttled down toward a suitable point on the slope to have a look at the inn while Nuri and her husband went up to their room.

"Honor shmonor," laughed Nuri, deliciously wicked, drawing "big fellow" out of his wrappings. "It's you I had to restore."

NOTES

A Riddle for a King

Called "Vasilisa the Priest's Daughter," in Aleksander Afanas'ev's collection of Russian folklore, *Russian Fairy Tales*, translated by Norbert Guterman (The Pantheon Fairy Tale and Folklore Library, New York, 1975). This tale appears in numerous anthologies including *The Virago Book of Fairy Tales*, ed. Angela Carter (Virago, 1991, p. 57).

Across the Sunlit Courtyard

This is Novella XI of Masuccio Salernitano's *Novellino* (1476). One of its fifty novelle is the early version of *Romeo and Juliet*, retold by Luigi Da Porto in 1530 as *Giulietta e Romeo* and versified in English in 1562 by Arthur Brooke in his *The Tragicall Historye of Romeus and Juliet*, which appears to be the blueprint for Shakespeare's celebrated version. Several of the novelle in the various collections feature a woman being forced into men's clothes (usually a monk's habit) in order to maintain her chastity.

In Straparola's *Nights of Pleasure*, a wife gets her own back on her jealous husband during a trip to a monastery. She arranges for her admirer to adopt the same disguise and on the couple's arrival invites them into a cell for food and wine. There the furious husband has to witness the admirer fawn over his wife; as a result he acknowledges his weakness and vows to be a more reasonable husband.

Secure, at Last

Based on "Bernabo of Genoa," Novella IX of Giovanni Boccaccio's *Decameron* (1349–51). The frame for the hundred stories of this collection is 1348, when ten young people, seven women and three men, leave Florence to flee to the hills of Fiesole in the hope of escaping the Black Death. To while away the time each one tells a story daily. These include bawdy tales, romances, adventures, fairy stories, and tales of wit and wisdom. Some of these were the basis of later plays, paintings, and operas.

These stories are often characterized by a ribaldry originating from fabliaux, and there are many tales of cross-dressing in the novelle collections in general. Of the first ten tales in the *Decameron*, three tell of women dressed as men.

Rubies for a Dog

This story appears in part one of *The Everyland Story Book*, ed. Oliver Brown (The Carey Press, 1931). This section is retold by the editor and called "Tales from Eastern Wonderlands." Judging from the other titles in the section, which include stories from the Indian epic *Mahabharata* as well as a tale of *Hatim Tai*, a legendary Arab hero, and also from a comment from the editor in the foreword, the story appears to have been collected in India, which was an exciting cauldron of tales from all the nations who settled there over the centuries. The names of the cities tell us that this one is set in Afghanistan.

The vast body of pan-Islamic tales found in India—from Iran, Afghanistan, Turkey, parts of Russia, Muslim Africa, and the Arabic-speaking countries—have yielded rich pickings for folklorists and collectors over the last couple of centuries. Many are part of a courtly tradition and appeared in verse form even earlier. Several others occur in the thirty-six or so volumes of the *Chronicles of Amir Hamza* (Dastan Amir Hamza) particularly in the section known as "The Spellbinding Talisman" (Tilism-e-Hoshruba).

The Legend of Mary Ambree

The ballad of Mary Ambree first appeared at the end of the sixteenth century. In her study *Warrior Women and Popular Balladry 1650–1850*, (Cambridge University Press, 1989), Dianne Dugaw describes it as a "pop hit" which went through all the stages of becoming a standard and eventually a "golden oldie" comparable in popularity during the seventeenth century to Bob Dylan's "Blowin' in the Wind" in the 1960s.

The story here is based on the text of "The valourous Acts performed at Gaunt, by the brave bonny Lasse Mary Ambree; Who in revenge of her Lovers death, did play her part most gallantly" (from a broadside *c.* 1640 in Manchester Central Library, Broadside Collection, Vol. 1) reproduced in *Warrior Women* (p. 37).

Mary's revelation at the end is the moment of truth symbolizing that in the end it was her woman's body that won her the battle.

The Mouse, the Thing, and the Wand

This tale is a transsexual fantasy. One European variant, ascribed to the Brothers Grimm, effectively suppresses all signs of the sexual "deviancy" implicit in the narrative by holding back the union of the women until after the heroine's transformation from female to male. My version is inspired by a variant a North-West Frontier guardsman told me when I was a girl in Pakistan. It was set in the Central Asian steppe and began as the heroine, dressed like a boy, restored the princess to her family. An almost identical version appears in *Armenian Folk-Tales and Fables* by Charles Downing (Oxford University Press, 1972). Both European and Armenian versions share the title "The Girl who became a Boy."

Like Pegasus, the winged horse of Greek mythology who helped the hero Bellerophon, the magical horse is a regular character in all the variants of this tale and also, in a less central role, in other cross-dressing tales. The fuller meaning of this consistent element of the tale type may be provided by depth psychology which regards beasts as symbols of the primitive urges of the human psyche, the sexual and bestial as well as the instinctual and wise. It is likely that the horse—generally a mare in these tales—represents the female aspect of the cross-dresser. In this tale the king commands Rahat to bring back a stallion to replace the mare. Perhaps together the mare and the stallion represent the bisexuality and the gender transformation in the story. In *The Dream and the Underworld* (Harper & Row, 1979, p. 146), James Hillman refutes the traditional hypothesis of depth psychology, suggesting instead that animals are gods. He sees them *"from an underworld perspective . . . as carriers of soul, perhaps totem carriers of our own free-soul or death-soul, there to help us see in the dark"*—which Rahat's mare certainly does. Hillman's thesis brings to mind the horses who draw the chariots of Hades—carriers of the dead—in this story, representing the death of the female within Rahat.

The Sand-Sifter

I reconstructed the story of Eugenia from fragments in *White Magic* by Charles Grant Loomis (Medieval Academy of America, Cambridge, Massachusetts, 1968), and *La Légende Dorée* by Teodor de Wyzewa (Librairie Académique Didier, 1902, p. 509) which is based on the Latin *Legenda Aurea* of Jacobus de Voragine (1230–98). Eugenia died around A.D. 258.

A Tortuous Path

E.T.C. Werner, the British consul in Foochow, China, writes of Princess Miao Shan's experiences in a substantial section entitled "The Goddess of Mercy" in *Myths and Legends of China* (Harrap, 1992). This includes, in much more detail, the experiences of the princess *en route* to deification.

Buddhism came to China through the oral tradition, during the Han dynasty (206 B.C.–220 C.E.) mainly via Central Asia, and over the years was modified to suit the local population. Taoist beliefs merged very swiftly with Buddhism and many of the gods held responsible for natural disaster—as well as for the easing of them—were co-opted into the faith. By the fourteenth century Taoism, Buddhism, and the Confucian faith had blended and it is the easy syncretism of the three that overlaid the folk beliefs of prerevelatory religion in China before communism.

Nine years—the time it took for Miao Shan to attain Perfection—are significant in Chinese Buddhism because it was for nine years that Bodhidharma, the first carrier of the faith to China, remained in contemplation, isolating himself by facing a blank wall. During this phase one of his disciples cut off his own arm to convince the Bodhidharma of his dedication. Miao Shan went on to become the much-loved Kuan-Yin, goddess of mercy and compassion, the most worshiped goddess in China today.

A Gown of Moonthreads

Stories of a merchant's prodigal son rescued by a princess are found all over the Jewish world. This version is based on Pinhas Sadeh's retelling in *Jewish Folktales* (Collins, 1990). I have interwoven it with fragments from "A Garment for the Moon" from *Miriam's Tambourine* by Howard Schwarz (Oxford University Press, 1988, p. 287) which is also about achieving the impossible, though on a different level.

The Merchant of Venice was almost certainly based on one of the variants—interestingly Shakespeare keeps the form of a Jewish money-lender and a non-Jewish savior heroine, though the hero has to be a Gentile to make the story acceptable to a Christian audience highly suspicious of Jews in a society where intermarriage was frowned upon even between Christians of different denominations.

What Will Be Will Be

The Reverend Charles Swynnerton collected this story in *Romantic Tales from the Panjab with Indian Nights' Entertainment* (Archibald Constable, 1908). He calls it "The Princess and the Ogres." It is part of the extensive pan-Islamic fairy tale corpus from Iran, Turkey, and the Arabic-speaking countries. I was virtually breast-fed on these stories and never weaned myself off them.

The Coward and the Heroine

Ralph Boggs's index to Spanish folklore refers this tale to *Manojico de Cuentos Fábulas apilogos, historietas y anecdotas (A Handful of Stories, Fables, Legends, and Anecdotes)* by M. Poloy Peyroton (Anufre, 1895, p. 163). The story here is based on Boggs's summary in which the tailor's wife does relieve him of the vest containing the money.

A Matter of Honor

Story VI "The Foolish Mussulmaun" from W. F. Connor's *Folktales from Tibet* (Hurst and Blackett, 1906) inspired this. I suspect that Connor chose his title because the simpleton of these stories is the famous Shaikh Chilli—a Muslim around whom many fables and stories cluster in the folklore of the Indo-Pakistani subcontinent.

About the Author

Shahrukh Husain, born and brought up in Pakistan, has studied myth and folklore from around the world for many years. She is the author of several children's books and a play for children, and has worked on film scripts for Merchant Ivory and Disney. A practicing psychotherapist, she is married with two children and lives in London.